THE CURIOSITREE

First published in Great Britain in 2016 by Wide Eyed Editions,
an imprint of Aurum Press, 74–77 White Lion Street, London N1 9PF
QuartoKnows.com
Visit our blogs at QuartoKnows.com

The Curiositree copyright © Aurum Press Ltd 2016
Illustrations copyright © Owen Davey 2016
Text copyright © Amanda Wood 2016
Concept, design and art direction by Mike Jolley

A catalogue record for this book is available from the British Library.

ISBN 978-1-84780-751-9

The illustrations were created digitally
Set in Gill Sans

 A Chapter Two book
created by Amanda Wood and Mike Jolley

Edited by Jenny Broom
Published by Rachel Williams
Consultants: Filipa Sampaio, Alex Coulton and David Gower

Manufactured in Dongguan, China TL012019

9 8 7 6

A Visual COMPENDIUM *of Wonders from Nature*

NATURAL WORLD

By Amanda Wood & Mike Jolley · *Illustrated by Owen Davey*

WIDE EYED EDITIONS

Editor's Note

ALBERT EINSTEIN ONCE FAMOUSLY SAID, "I HAVE NO SPECIAL TALENTS. I AM ONLY PASSIONATELY CURIOUS." Curiosity, Einstein understood, has led to humankind's greatest discoveries, breakthroughs and achievements. It is a quality that we have in abundance; from the very moment that we are born we are driven to explore and explain the living world around us.

And what rewards our curiosity brings! For our planet is rich with oceans, forests, deserts, mountains, and creatures of every kind…

The more we explore the natural world, the more we uncover its boggling complexity. And the more we strive to comprehend the workings of nature, the more we see the interconnectedness between creatures and the environments they inhabit. The natural world is inextricably linked.

We now understand that over millions of years, since life appeared on Earth, each animal and every plant has evolved to look, behave and procreate in the way that gives it its best chance of survival: every tree's leaf and bird's feather is exquisitely designed for a particular purpose, and to work in harmony with its environment. This book is designed to help you explore and understand these connections, and to celebrate the extraordinary resourcefulness and resilience of the natural world.

Another great man, Mark Twain, once said, "Truth is stranger than fiction." You only have to turn to the 'peculiar platypus' on page 84, or take a look at the 'creatures of the deep' on page 93 to see that this is the case! But the strangest truth of all, perhaps, is that just as humankind begins to uncover the natural world's most intriguing secrets, we threaten its very existence. The challenge for humans now is to find ways to live and survive in harmony with nature, and curiosity will provide the answers to these challenges. So, set out on your own adventure in this book, and discover why the natural world is worthy of your unending curiosity.

Contents

Example 1

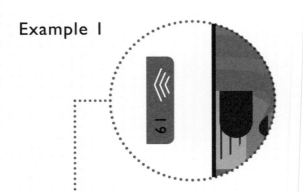

Follow the arrows and chart numbers...

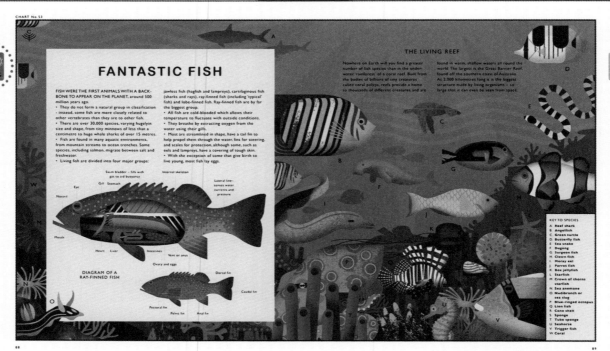

Example 2

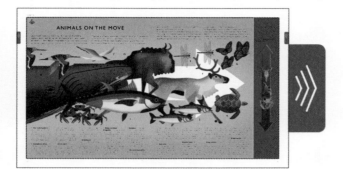
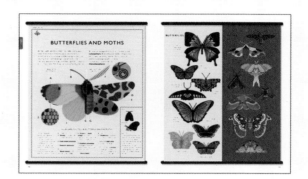

Introduction

EVERY TIME YOU OPEN THIS BOOK, you can go on a different journey of discovery to find out more about the natural world and its many wonderful inhabitants.

All of the charts in this book are colour-coded according to the subject matter:

Yellow charts tell you about **habitats** or environments.

Orange charts focus on particular **species** or groups of plants and animals.

Blue charts look at animal behaviour or special **adaptations** that help living things in their constant fight for survival.

If you like, you can simply start the book at the beginning and continue reading until you get to the end. Use the coloured ribbons like a bookmark, or to mark your place so you can return to pages that you found especially interesting.

Alternatively, open the book wherever you like (you could even start right at the back) and then look for the coloured arrows that you'll find in the left and right margins of each double-page spread. They'll take you backwards or forwards to other charts in the book containing information that is connected in some way to what you have just read.

Be curious, follow the arrows and find out something new on every journey you take.

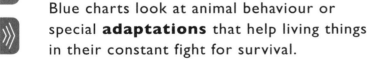

LIVING THINGS

THE WORLD IS FULL OF LIVING THINGS – from giant whales to tiny bugs, majestic redwood trees to colourful fungi. Although they may look very different from one another, most of the plants and animals with which we are most familiar share certain basic characteristics.

MOVEMENT

Animals are usually easy to identify from other life forms because they can move – either the whole or parts of their bodies.

Different creatures have evolved many different forms of movement, from swimming fish, flying birds and hopping frogs, to the those that can walk and run – as humans do. However, while this rule is true for most land animals many creatures that live in water may spend all of their adults lives in one place and have trailing body parts that make them appear more like plants, for example coral polyps.

Plants are able to move too. They cannot move from place to place but they can turn their leaves towards light, open their flower petals to the sun, and send roots towards water.

REPRODUCTION

For all living things, the drive to reproduce is one of the strongest instincts of all. Animals can be successful in many ways – growing and feeding in order to survive themselves – but if they do not produce offspring then they will have failed to ensure the survival of their species on Earth.

Animals reproduce in many different ways. Some give birth to live young, others lay eggs, while some sprout babies like buds out of their own bodies – as is the case with sponges and some types of jellyfish for example. Plants reproduce in different ways too: some send out spores or seeds (such as an oak tree, which produces acorns), while others send out special roots from which new plants can grow.

RESPONSE

Most animals are highly complex and extremely responsive compared to other forms of life, using their senses to tell them what is happening in the world around them.

Even the simplest creatures can react quickly to changes in their environment – reaching out for food or shrinking away from danger. Those with well-developed nervous systems can go one step further – by learning from their experiences, adapting their behaviour or appearance to increase their chances of success. This ability is unique to the animal world.

Plants too can sense the environment around them, sending their roots down into the soil to find water or their stems upwards towards light.

NUTRITION

All living things need energy to carry on living. Plants can make their own food using the energy from the sun to produce glucose, which they store in their cells as starch. Most other organisms need to eat plants or animals, or both, in order to obtain energy and many have developed incredibly specialised ways of finding, catching and digesting their food. Cows, for example, have four stomachs in order to process as much goodness as they can from the grass they eat. Some snakes can swallow whole animals many times larger than themselves, taking months to digest their victim before they need to eat again, whereas shrews have fast metabolisms, which means they need to eat almost constantly in order to stay alive.

DEAD OR ALIVE

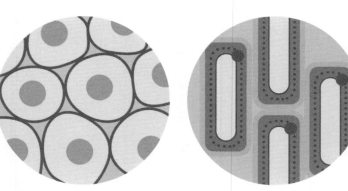

Animal cells

Plant cells

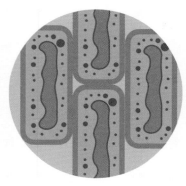

Dead plant cells

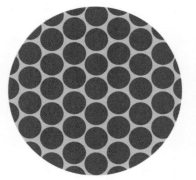

Particles

All living things are made from one or more cells, often with millions of them working together to make up a whole organism. Even when something dies, you can still see its cells under a microscope, whether it's the wood of a chair that was once a living tree or the leather of a shoe that was once the skin of a living animal. Things that have never been alive are not made of cells but of tiny things called particles.

RESPIRATION

In animals, we typically refer to respiration as 'breathing'. Respiration is a chemical reaction that releases energy. It occurs in every cell of a living organism. In most animals, aerobic respiration uses oxygen breathed in through the lungs to react with glucose in the blood to produce the energy needed for growth, repair and movement. Water and carbon dioxide are produced as bi-products and need to be excreted. In plant cells respiration uses glucose combined with oxygen to release energy just as animal cells do.

EXCRETION

Although respiration produces energy, it also produces bi-products which all organisms must dispose of in order to remain healthy. An animal's lungs excrete carbon dioxide as it breathes out, its kidneys remove nitrogen waste from its body as urine and it may shed excess salt by sweating. Plants excrete oxygen and water through their leaves.

Most creatures also produce another type of waste – faeces – but this is not a bi-product of a metabolic process so it is expelled from the body rather than excreted.

GROWTH

Babies grow into adults and seedlings grow into bigger plants, but the process of growing can be very different among living organisms.

Most mammals grow until they reach adulthood and their skeletons grow with them, each bone getting bigger over time. Many invertebrates can only grow by shedding their hard outer skeleton and growing a new, larger version. Other creatures, like butterflies, grow by changing shape completely, transforming into their adult shape through a process called metamorphosis.

THE LIVING WORLD

ALL ORGANISMS CAN BE CLASSIFIED INTO GROUPS ACCORDING TO HOW CLOSELY THEY ARE RELATED TO EACH OTHER. These groups are then arranged into different levels, as shown opposite. The two most familiar groups – animals and plants – contain the multi-celled complex organisms that make up most of the obvious life of our planet. All life forms are then further divided into groups that share increasingly similar characteristics until you arrive at a single species.

The science of classifying forms, **taxonomy**, also identifies all species by giving them a Latin name. Whereas an animal may have a number of different common names, its Latin name is fixed. The puma, cougar, mountain lion and catamount are all one and the same creature – *Puma concolor*.

With new facts about the life of our planet constantly coming to light, and new species still being discovered, the job of taxonomists is never complete. Because life in all its infinite variety does not always fit neatly into man-made patterns of organisation, new discoveries (such as loriciferans – a whole new phylum of tiny creatures identified relatively recently in the 1980s) sometimes lead to major revisions of the existing system.

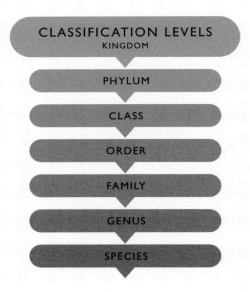

In the world of invertebrates there are many minor phyla in addition to those that contain familiar creatures such as insects or snails. Many of these animals are microscopic, such as the rotifers or tardigrades, and while some such phyla contain only a handful of species, a few contain many thousands.

HOW MANY LIVING ANIMALS?

Nearly two million animal species have already been formally described, but scientists believe that there are many more waiting to be discovered – perhaps as many as 7 million. Of those we do already know about, only about 5 per cent are vertebrates. The biggest group of creatures are the invertebrates, with insects being the most abundant of these, both in number of species and in quantity of individuals.

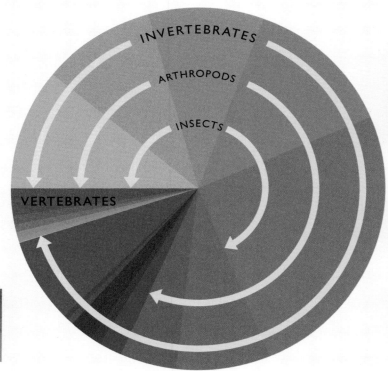

VERTEBRATES 4.8%
Broken down into:
Fish
Birds
Reptiles
Amphibians
Mammals

INVERTEBRATES 95.2%
Broken down into:
Molluscs
Sponges
Cnidariuns
Flatworms
Segmented worms
Roundworms
Other invertebrates
Arthropods

ARTHROPODS
Broken down into:
Crustaceans
Centipedes, millepedes
Arachnids
Insects

INSECTS
Broken down into:
Beetles
Bees, wasps, ants, sawflies
Butterflies, moths
Flies
Other insects

EXAMPLE: CLASSIFICATION OF THE GREY WOLF

The diagram below shows all the groups to which the grey wolf belongs.

KINGDOM:
Animalia
Contains all animals identified on Earth so far, from insects and molluscs to birds and mammals.

PHYLUM:
Chordata
Includes all animals with backbones, called vertebrates.

CLASS:
Mammalia
Contains all vertebrates that suckle their young.

ORDER:
Carnivora
A single lineage of several families of generally dog-like and cat-like mammals.

FAMILY:
Canidae
Contains dogs and their closest relatives – wolves, jackals and foxes.

GENUS:
Canis
Contains approximately ten living species – the dogs, wolves and jackals.

SPECIES:
Canis lupus
Contains only one species – the grey wolf. Some biologists also classify domesticated dogs under this species name; others classify them as *Canis familiaris*.

In summary the wolf is of the kingdom Animalia, the phylum Chordata, the class Mammalia, the order Carnivora, the family Canidae, the genus *Canis* and the species *Canis lupus*. All living things can be classified in this way.

A GUIDE TO ANIMAL

NEARLY TWO MILLION ANIMAL SPECIES HAVE BEEN IDENTIFIED BY SCIENTISTS, but most animals can be divided into either vertebrates (animals with a backbone) or invertebrates (animals with no backbone). Similarly, plants can be split into those that flower and those that don't. You can see the main groups of animals and plants within each division in the

PLANTS

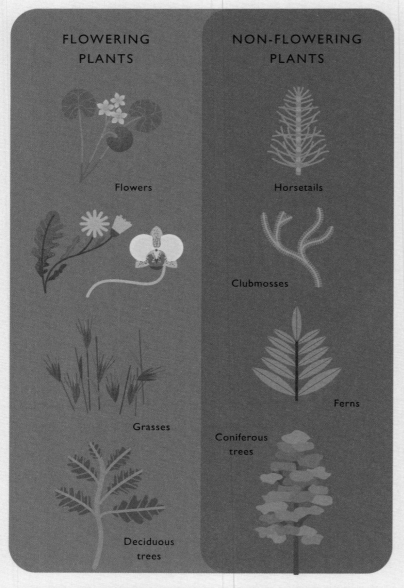

FLOWERING PLANTS

Flowers

Grasses

Deciduous trees

NON-FLOWERING PLANTS

Horsetails

Clubmosses

Ferns

Coniferous trees

MOSSES AND LIVERWORTS

INVERTEBRATES
(no backbone)

Flatworms

Roundworms

Segmented worms

Sponges

Echinoderms

Crustaceans

Cnidarians

Molluscs

Myriapods

Arachnids

Insects

AND PLANT GROUPS

chart below. Our knowledge of how these different groups of living things relate to one another has changed over time as new discoveries help us to better understand the evolutionary links that show how life on Earth has evolved over millions of years. Some invertebrates, for example, are more closely related to vertebrates than they are to other invertebrates!

ANIMALS

VERTEBRATES
(have a backbone)

Fish

Amphibians

Reptiles

Birds

Mammals

OTHER LIFE FORMS

There are many living organisms that do not fit in with the divisions or main groups shown opposite. Fungi, for example, were once classified as plants but now occupy a separate kingdom of their own.

Fungi

Many microscopic life forms also have their own groups. You can see some of these creatures below. Some biologists also consider viruses to be living organisms even though they do not share many of the characteristics that define other living things.

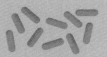

Bacteria

Protozoa   Algae

There are still completely new forms of life being discovered, particularly among the world of marine invertebrates. This loriciferan is one species of a whole new phylum only recently discovered.

Loriciferan

Material for nest building

A

B

Plenty of places to hide among the branches

Trees to nest in

G

PINE TREE

Bark full of burrowing beetles and other insects

C

OAK TREE

E

Undergrowth for shelter

Plenty of food in the form of nuts, seeds, buds, flowers and leaves

F

Damp leaf litter full of juicy worms and other invertebrates

Pine cone

Acorn

Damp banks where soft-bodied creatures won't dry out

Water for drinking and as a place to lay eggs

D

STREAM

WHAT IS A HABITAT?

ON THE SIMPLEST LEVEL, A HABITAT IS WHERE AN ANIMAL OR PLANT LIVES. There are many different kinds of habitat – from lush tropical forests and windswept prairies to the teeming life of a coral reef. For some creatures a habitat might be as restricted as a rotting log or a temporary pool that forms after rain falls in the desert.

In its widest sense, however, a habitat includes not just the setting in which living things are found but the group of plants and animals that typically choose to live there. A habitat defined in this way is known as an **ecosystem**. Every habitat has something different to offer. Some, like the temperate woodland shown opposite, are rich in both food and shelter, and, as a consequence, many different kinds of

animal and plant live here, but even in the most inhospitable places – whether the hottest desert or the highest mountain – nature finds a way for life to exist.

In all habitats, the plants and animals that live there have adapted over time to increase their chances of survival, developing features to suit the environment in which they live. Some creatures are so highly evolved to survive in a particular place that they can no longer live anywhere else.

This woodland glade has plenty to offer the abundance of creatures that live there. Take a look below at some of the adaptations that allow each animal to make the most of their habitat.

A. **Crossbill** – The tips of this finch's beak overlap, which makes it an ideal tool for opening tough pine cones to get at the nutricious seeds inside.

B. **Pine marten** – This creature spends much of its time in trees and has semi-retractable claws to help it climb and run along branches in search of prey.

C. **Woodpecker's** – With its chisel-like bill and hard skull, this bird hammers away tree bark to find food and hollow out a nesting site in a tree trunk.

D. **Frog** – A frog's long legs and webbed feet, which act like flippers, help it to swim. Its wide mouth and sticky tongue are ideal for catching invertebrates.

E. **Fallow deer** – This deer's spotted coat camouflages it in the dappled shade of the trees. The position of its eyes gives it good all-round vision.

F. **Wild boar** – This creature, and especially its young, is well camouflaged among the undergrowth. Its elongated snout is ideal for sniffing out and digging up small invertebrates, nuts and roots from deep within the leaf litter.

G. **Grey squirrel** – With strong teeth ideal for gnawing through tough acorn shells, long claws to help it climb trees and a bushy tail for balance, this creature spends most of its time up in the branches. It makes its nest of leaves high in a tree.

BIODIVERSITY

Biodiversity is a term that generally refers to the variety and variability of life on Earth. Different habitats show great variation in the number of species that live there. In some places, like reefs or rainforests, living things are so abundant that huge numbers of species live side by side. In more challenging environments, like, for example, the polar regions, the number of species present may be smaller – there may be only a few hundred species of insect living there, compared to millions in a rainforest.

However, what these inhospitable habitats may lack in biodiversity, they often make up for in sheer population numbers: in the seas around Antarctica tens of millions of crabeater seals can be found – the most numerous large mammals on earth.

TEMPERATE BROADLEAF AND MIXED FOREST

These forests generally have a mild climate and plenty of rain throughout the year. The trees are mainly deciduous and drop their leaves in the winter, forming a deep layer of litter which supports its own complex web of life. In warmer parts of the zone, trees and plants such as eucalyptus and bamboo form evergreen forests.

Example species (deciduous forest): Fallow deer, badger, woodpecker; oak, beech, maple
Example species (evergreen forest): Koala, panda; eucalyptus, bamboo

2

POLAR ICE AND TUNDRA

The Arctic and Antarctic are the coldest places on Earth, with 24-hour daylight in summer and perpetual darkness in winter. There is little vegetation and few animals live on the land. The stormy polar seas, in contrast, are rich in life, from minute plankton to giant whales.

Example species: Polar bear, walrus, blue whale; lichen, moss

CHART No.5

WORLD HABITATS

THE EARTH HAS A COMPLEX JIGSAW OF HABITATS. This is thanks partly to its great physical variety – from towering mountains to desert plains, mighty rivers to inland seas – but it is also climate that determines the plants and animals that live in any given place. This world map shows nine of the major world habitats. Each supports its own specially adapted community of plants and animals.

NORTH AMERICA

Tropic of Cancer

Atlantic Ocean

Equator

Pacific Ocean

SOUTH AMERICA

Tropic of Capricorn

- 1. Temperate broadleaf and mixed forest
- 2. Polar ice and tundra
- 3. Hot desert
- 4. Mountain
- 5. Grassland
- 6. Coniferous forest
- 7. Tropical forest
- 8. Wetland
- 9. Ocean

CONIFEROUS FOREST

Short summers and long, cold winters are the key features of these forests that stretch across the top of North America, Europe and Asia, also known as boreal forests or taiga. Many animals sleep through the winter months here, while others remain active, feeding on food stores made earlier in the year.

Example species: Brown bear, long-eared owl, grey wolf; spruce, pine, larch

6

TROPICAL FOREST

Near the equator it is always warm and humid, an ideal climate in which plants can grow all year round. The forests that grow here contain the richest variety of life on land: perhaps half of all the different kinds of plant and animal in the world live here.

Example species: Toucan, howler monkey, green tree frog; teak, orchid, liana

7

HOT DESERT

3

While deserts can also be cold, scorching heat and lack of rain make hot deserts one of the harshest places to live on Earth. There are few plants but despite this many animals have adapted to live here, conserving water in their bodies and becoming active only at dawn and dusk.

Example species: Camel, jerboa, horned viper; cactus

MOUNTAIN

4

Mountains cover nearly 25 per cent of the Earth's surface in both warm and cold regions of the world. The animals and plants that live on the higher slopes above the treeline have adapted to harsh conditions: low oxygen, sparse vegetation, low humidity, cold temperatures and often strong winds.

Example species: Eagle, snow leopard, ibex; sedge grass, lichen, moss

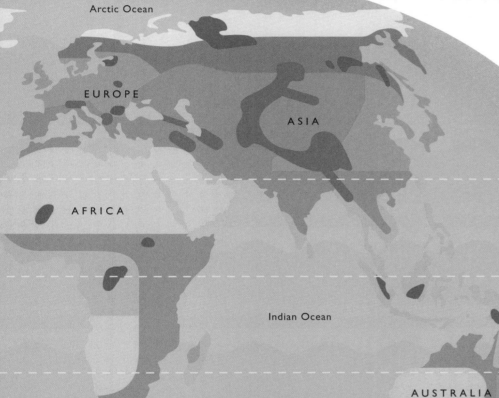

Arctic Ocean

EUROPE

ASIA

AFRICA

Indian Ocean

AUSTRALIA

Southern Ocean

ANTARCTICA

5

GRASSLAND

Stretching across the wide plains of temperate and tropical regions, grasslands form where it is too dry for many trees to grow. Grasses are the main plant growing there and there is little shelter. In the tropical grasslands of Africa, the savannah, great herds of plant-eaters, such as antelopes and wildebeest, provide food for a great variety of predators, including lions and cheetahs, and scavengers like hyenas and vultures.

The prairies and pampas of the Americas and the steppes of Asia are examples of cooler grasslands.

Example species (tropical): Lion, zebra, elephant, ostrich; grass, acacia
Example species (temperate): Bison, mongoose; grass, mesquite, saltbush

WETLAND

8

About a third of the water in our atmosphere returns to the ocean by flowing over or beneath the surface of the land. In doing so, it supports all land-based life and creates a diverse set of habitats – from highland streams and mighty rivers to salt marshes and tropical swamps – that provides homes for a huge variety of plant and animal life, particularly birds and insects.
(Only major wetland areas are shown above.)

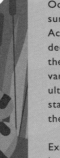

Example species: Frog, beaver, heron, pike, dragonfly; reeds, water lily, mangrove

OCEAN

9

Oceans cover 70 per cent of the world's surface and are where life on Earth began. Across a wide range of habitats – from deep ocean trenches to sunlit coral reefs – the oceans support a great number and variety of creatures, but most life here ultimately depends on plankton – the starting point for the great food web of the seas.

Example species: Butterfly fish, dolphin, herring; krill, plankton, kelp

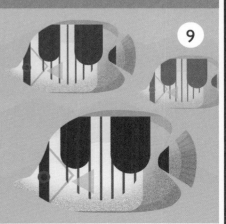

CHART No.6

THE FIGHT F

IN THE NATURAL WORLD EVERYTHING HAS A PURPOSE. The colourful feathers of a male bird of paradise are there to help him attract a mate, the shape of a guillemot's egg is designed to stop it rolling away off the edge of a cliff, the patterned wings of a butterfly helps it frighten away predators – everywhere you look, living organisms have adapted and evolved, whether in appearance or behaviour, to maximise their chances of survival.

Over many generations these adaptations have come about through small variations that have allowed one living thing to compete better for survival than another. As an example, the giraffes with the longest necks can reach the

OR SURVIVAL

most food so are more likely to survive when food is scarce and go on to produce long-necked offspring of their own.

Adaptations that help living things survive can take a number of forms — physical, (such as an animal's shape),

behavioural (such as the ability to use tools) or physiological (such as the ability to make venom). Over time, they can help an animal survive in more challenging environments with little food and harsh climates, such as deserts or mountaintops.

Plants too have adapted to increase their chances of survival, from the cacti's ability to store water, to the myriad ways in which plants spread their seeds. Nowhere can nature's ingenuity be seen more clearly than in the fight to survive.

Flying fox

Badger

Civet

Pika

Beaver

AMAZING MAMMALS,

THIS GROUP OF VERTEBRATES CONTAINS SOME OF THE BEST-KNOWN AND MOST STUDIED SPECIES ON EARTH, and is the class to which we humans, *Homo sapiens*, also belong.

• There are over 5,000 species of mammal: a hugely varied and complex collection that includes our largest living land and sea creatures – the African elephant and blue whale respectively.

• The first mammals appeared around 195 million years ago. They evolved from early reptile-like animals and were small, shrew-like creatures.

• Since then, mammals have adapted to live in many of the world's habitats – in the air, in both fresh and salt water and underground – although they are at their most widespread and diverse on land.

• One reason for the success of mammals is that they are warm-blooded, which means they can maintain a stable body temperature. This allows them to remain active even if their environment is very cold or very hot.

• Many mammals are also highly adaptable, and able to modify their behaviour in reaction to a change in circumstances. This ability has allowed them to colonise even the harshest

Dromedary camel

Wildebeest

Polar bear

Lion

Jerboa

Echidna

Fennec fox

Red panda

Aardvark

Marmot

GREAT AND SMALL

environments, evolving new bodily features and behaviours that help them survive even in extreme conditions.

• There are three main kinds of living mammal: monotremes (for example, the echidnas and platypus) marsupials (for example, koalas and kangaroos) and placental mammals, of which the latter is by far the most common today.

• With the exception of the monotremes that lay eggs, mammals give birth to live young. All living mammals nourish their young on milk produced by the female's mammary glands – the unique physical feature which gives this class its name.

• Most living mammals have a covering of hair on their bodies, though this may vary considerably in appearance between species, from the thick fur of the polar bear to the bristles of a warthog or the modified hairs of a porcupine's spines.

Pipistrelle bat

Giraffe

Snow leopard

Babirusa

Silvery gibbon

Addax

Jackrabbit

Lemming

SKELETONS AND SKULLS

ALL MAMMALS HAVE THE SAME BASIC SKELETON. Although they may look very different, a giraffe has the same number of neck bones as a human being, and a cat – despite being much larger – has a similar bone structure to that of a mouse. Around this bony framework many different body shapes have evolved, reflecting the lifestyle, habitat and diet of each particular species.

SKULLS AND TEETH

The jaws of modern mammals have evolved some important characteristics. Their lower jaw is hinged directly to the rest of the skull and is made from a single piece of bone. Strong muscles allow for complex movements, and the mouth is equipped with specialised teeth that reflect the animal's diet. All of these things help to make mammals effective eating machines.

• Most mammals have four types of teeth: **incisors** for biting and cutting; **canines** for gripping and tearing; and cheek teeth (**premolars** and **molars**) for crushing and grinding.

• The shape, size and arrangement of these teeth vary according to the food an animal eats. We can often tell a great deal about the lifestyle and behaviour of an extinct creature from nothing more than a handful of its teeth or skull fragments.

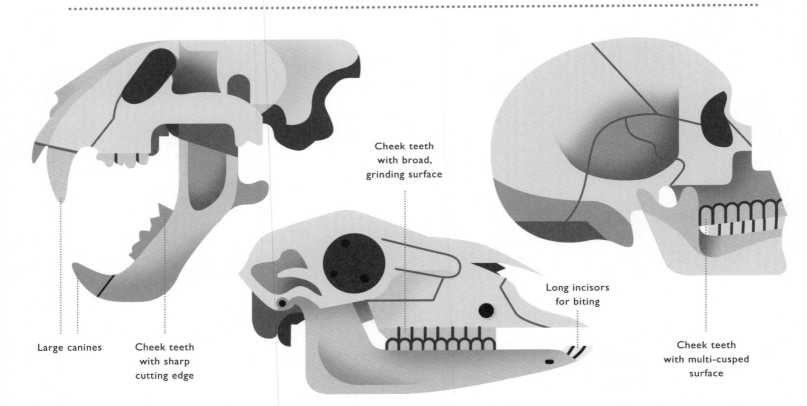

Cheek teeth with broad, grinding surface

Long incisors for biting

Large canines

Cheek teeth with sharp cutting edge

Cheek teeth with multi-cusped surface

CARNIVORE SKULL
Meat-eaters have teeth shaped for tearing with large canines for ripping and gripping prey, and skulls equipped with powerful jaw muscles capable of biting with great force. They also have sharp-edged cheek teeth used to shred meat and crack open bones.

HERBIVORE SKULL
Plant-eaters have teeth equipped to chew tough vegetation, with jaws that can typically move from side to side as well as up and down to crush food. Most do not have canine teeth, but have long, sharp incisors for snipping off foliage, and broad cheek teeth.

OMNIVORE SKULL
Creatures (including humans) that eat both plants and animals have skulls and teeth suitable for chewing a wide range of foods. Their cheek teeth often have a number of raised points, or cusps, designed to cope with processing a varied diet.

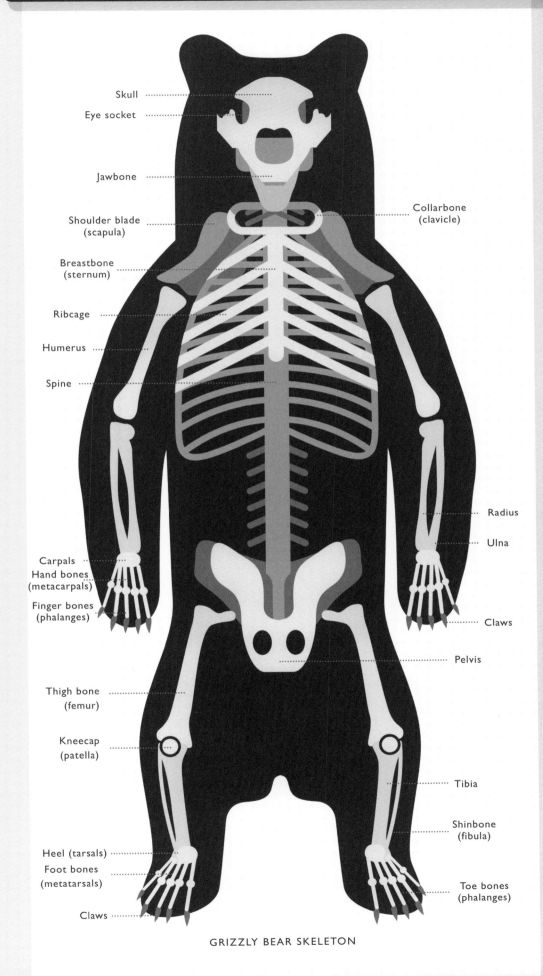

Skull

Eye socket

Jawbone

Shoulder blade
(scapula)

Breastbone
(sternum)

Ribcage

Humerus

Spine

Carpals
Hand bones
(metacarpals)

Finger bones
(phalanges)

Thigh bone
(femur)

Kneecap
(patella)

Heel (tarsals)
Foot bones
(metatarsals)

Claws

Collarbone
(clavicle)

Radius

Ulna

Claws

Pelvis

Tibia

Shinbone
(fibula)

Toe bones
(phalanges)

GRIZZLY BEAR SKELETON

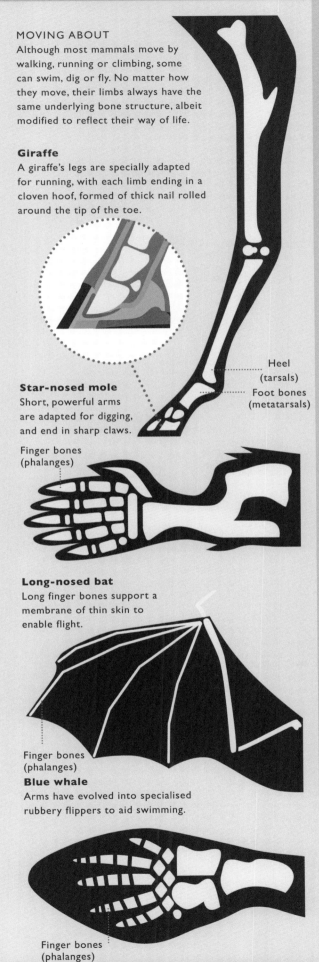

MOVING ABOUT

Although most mammals move by walking, running or climbing, some can swim, dig or fly. No matter how they move, their limbs always have the same underlying bone structure, albeit modified to reflect their way of life.

Giraffe

A giraffe's legs are specially adapted for running, with each limb ending in a cloven hoof, formed of thick nail rolled around the tip of the toe.

Heel
(tarsals)
Foot bones
(metatarsals)

Star-nosed mole

Short, powerful arms are adapted for digging, and end in sharp claws.

Finger bones
(phalanges)

Long-nosed bat

Long finger bones support a membrane of thin skin to enable flight.

Finger bones
(phalanges)

Blue whale

Arms have evolved into specialised rubbery flippers to aid swimming.

Finger bones
(phalanges)

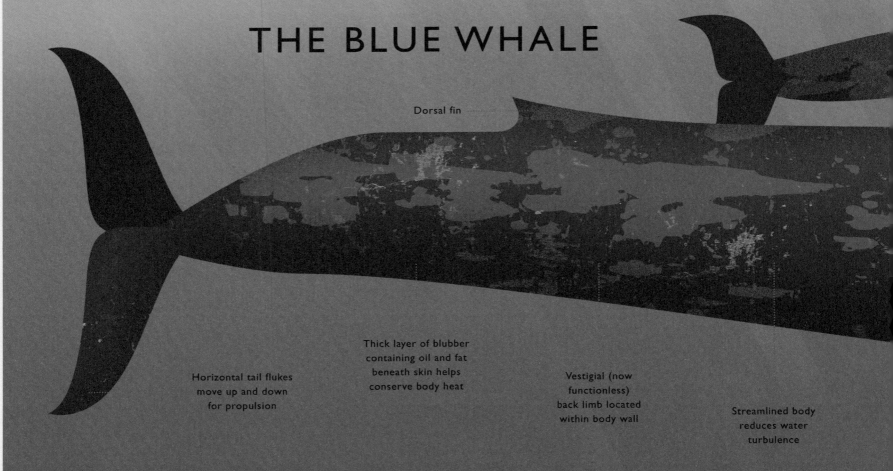

THE BLUE WHALE

Dorsal fin

Horizontal tail flukes move up and down for propulsion

Thick layer of blubber containing oil and fat beneath skin helps conserve body heat

Vestigial (now functionless) back limb located within body wall

Streamlined body reduces water turbulence

NOT ONLY IS THE BLUE WHALE THE LARGEST LIVING CREATURE – IT IS THE BIGGEST ANIMAL EVER TO HAVE EXISTED ON EARTH. Despite its superficially fish-like appearance, it belongs to a class of mammals known as **cetaceans** that includes whales, dolphins and porpoises.

• A fully-grown adult whale can reach over 33 metres in length, longer than three double-decker buses.

• It is one of the most specialised of all mammals with its fish-shaped body and flipper-like front limbs, and is an example of a **baleen whale**, named after the hundreds of horny (baleen) plates found on either side of its upper jaw. It uses these to sieve thousands of tiny planktonic crustaceans, such as krill, from seawater.

• Like all true mammals, the blue whale is warm-blooded and it gives birth to a single calf that it then suckles for six to

FEEDING

To feed, the blue whale gulps a huge mouthful of seawater, expanding its lower jaw into a giant bag that can hold more than 90 tonnes of food and water. This food sticks to fine bristles on the baleen plates when the water is expelled. It is estimated that a blue whale can eat as many as 40 million krill in a single day!

Krill

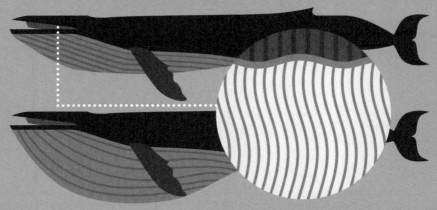

Throat grooves

Baleen plates

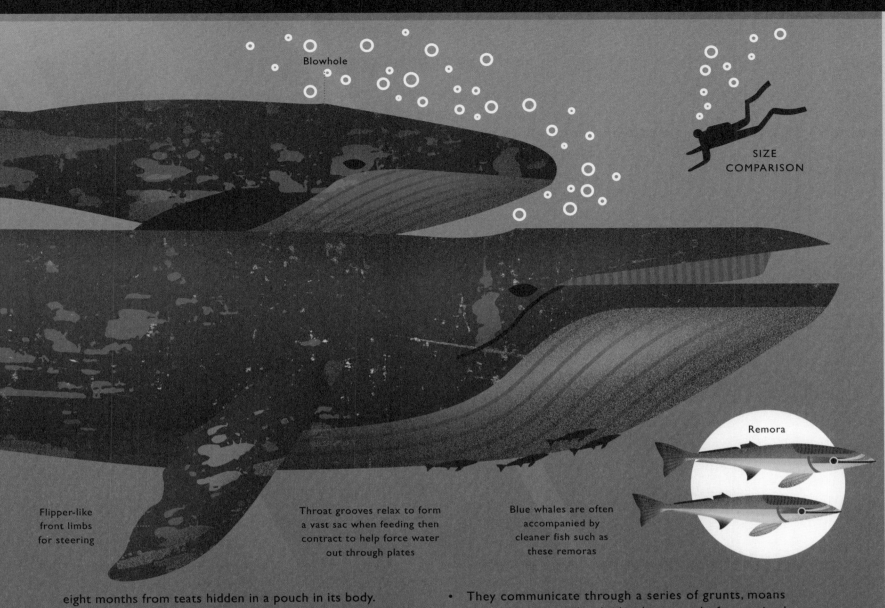

SIZE
COMPARISON

Blowhole

Remora

Flipper-like
front limbs
for steering

Throat grooves relax to form
a vast sac when feeding then
contract to help force water
out through plates

Blue whales are often
accompanied by
cleaner fish such as
these remoras

eight months from teats hidden in a pouch in its body.
• A whale calf may be as long as 7 metres at birth and
will drink over 400 litres of its mother's milk every day
until it starts to feed for itself.
• A migratory species, blue whales are found in all of
the world's oceans. They feed in the Arctic and Antarctic
during the summer when krill are plentiful and move to
tropical water to breed during the winter.

• They communicate through a series of grunts, moans
and hums and can make the loudest sound of any animal,
echoing through the ocean at 180 decibels.
• Whales breathe through nostrils known as **blowholes**
on the top of their heads. Strong muscles keep these
closed when the whale is underwater, opening when the
whale surfaces to explosively release air from its lungs
before taking another breath.

Bottlenose
dolphin

TOOTHED WHALES

The remaining members of the
cetaceans are the **toothed whales** –
the dolphins, orca and porpoises as
well as the sperm, white and beaked
whales. Toothed whales make up
almost 90 per cent of living cetaceans
and all possess teeth rather than
baleen plates, often housed in a long
beak-like snout at the front of the head.

MICRO-CREATURES

MICRO-CREATURES – ANIMALS THAT ARE TOO SMALL TO BE STUDIED BY THE NAKED EYE – FORM A LARGE PART OF THE ANIMAL KINGDOM. However small they are, and some are very small indeed, most have a recognisable body plan that can be used to help classify them.

• Many micro-creatures live in water or in damp places on land. Some live in the soil, or in the dust that accumulates in our houses. Others live on other animals – and that includes us humans!

• Some, like the **tardigrades** and **rotifers**, are built to survive harsh conditions. They can shrivel to nothing more than a dried-up husk, sometimes remaining like this for decades, and then come back to life again when they come into contact with water.

• Many micro-creatures form part of the diverse group of organisms known as **plankton** – a vital source of food for many aquatic species such as fish and whales.

• Scientists believe that there are many more species of micro-creatures yet to be discovered.

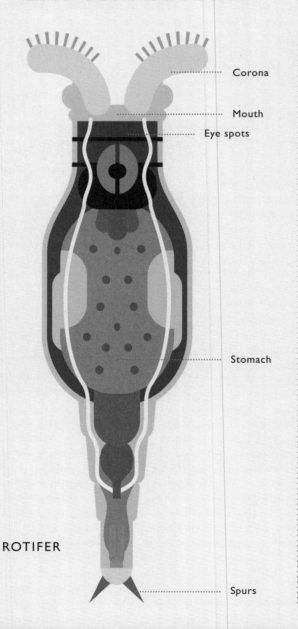

Corona
Mouth
Eye spots
Stomach
ROTIFER
Spurs

KEY TO SPECIES

A **Tardigrade** – up to 0.5mm
Also known as water bears or moss piglets, tardigrades have dagger-like teeth and four pairs of stubby legs ending in claws known as disks. They live in damp habitats on land as well as in water, and are commonly found among mosses and lichens where they feed on plant cells and microscopic invertebrates. Tardigrades can survive extreme conditions – they have been found to withstand temperatures from just above absolute zero to higher than the boiling point of water, pressure greater than in the deepest ocean trench, radiation far higher than the lethal dose for humans, and even a vacuum in outer space!

B. **Copepod** – up to 2mm
These tiny crustaceans are found in all types of water where they feed on phytoplankton (microscopic plants). Many have exoskeletons that are almost transparent.

C. **Eyelash mite** – up to 0.4mm
These tiny parasitic mites typically live in the hair follicles of human eyelashes and eyebrows. Their bodies are covered in scales to help them anchor inside an individual follicle where they then eat skin cells with their tiny pin-like mouthparts.

D. **Cladocera** – up to 6mm
Commonly called water fleas, these crustaceans are most often found in inland waters. Their eggs have a protective outer layer that preserves the contents from harsh environmental conditions such as drought. They are so small that they can be dispersed by the wind over great distances.

E. **Loricifera** – up to 1mm
These minute marine creatures are members of a whole new phylum of animals only discovered in the 1980s. They can be found in marine sediment worldwide, where they attach themselves to individual grains of sand.

F. **House dust mite** – up to 0.3mm
These tiny mites live alongside humans, particularly in carpets, mattresses and bedding. They survive in all climates and feed on our dead skin and other minute particles of organic matter. One gramme of dust can contain as many as 500 mites and, together with their droppings, they are a common cause of asthma and allergies in humans.

G. **Rotifer** – up to 3mm
Occurring in their thousands in all kinds of aquatic habitats, these so-called 'wheel-animals' are most common in fresh water where they are an important part of the zooplankton (plankton formed from animals). There are a variety of different shapes of rotifer but all have hair-like cilia on their heads, called the corona, which they use to sweep food into their mouths.

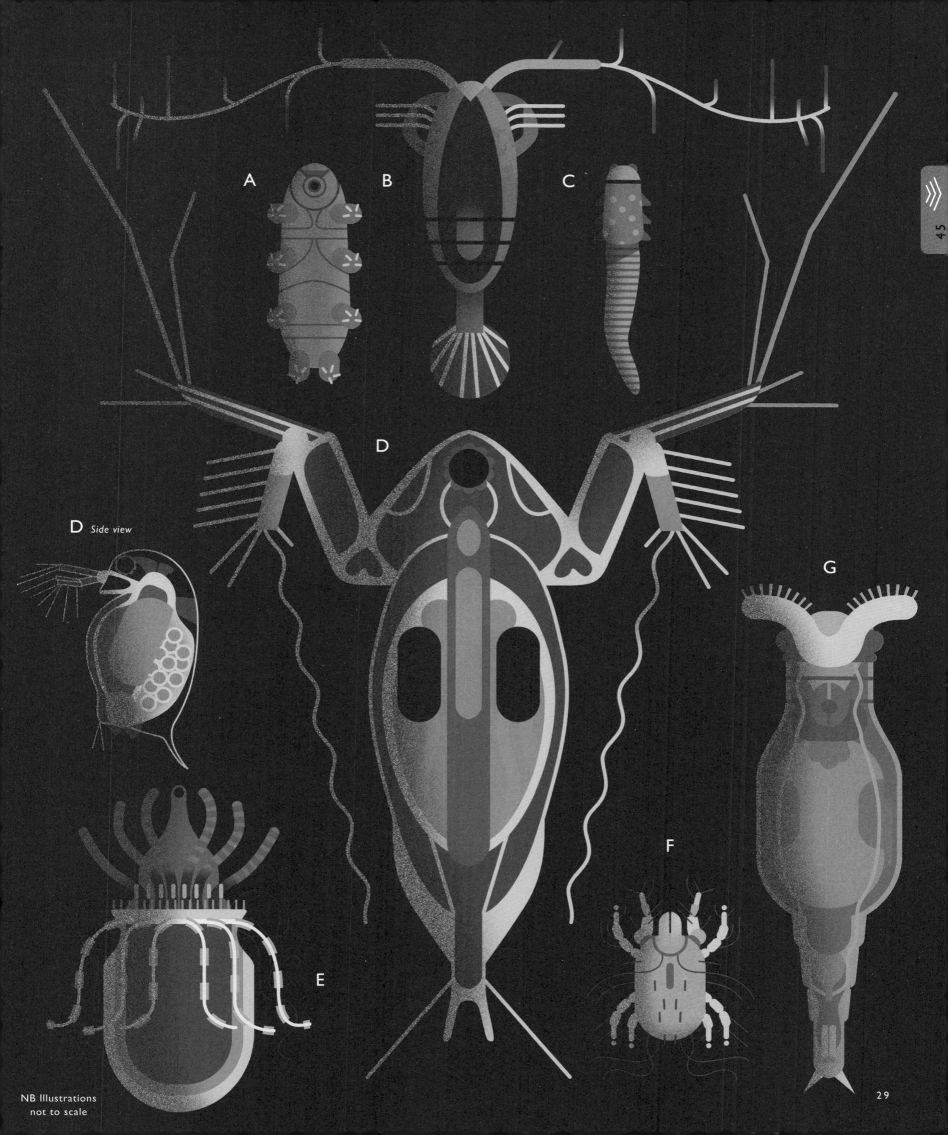

A

B

C

D

D *Side view*

E

F

G

NB Illustrations
not to scale

ANIMALS ON THE MOVE

WHETHER CHASING THE SUN OR CHASING THE RAIN, MANY CREATURES MOVE FROM ONE PLACE TO ANOTHER AT PARTICULAR TIMES OF THE YEAR. Sometimes these journeys, known as migrations, cover thousands of miles, others, only a few.

They typically happen every year, linked to the cycle of the seasons, and may involve travel through the air, over land or across oceans.
• There are different reasons why animals migrate. They may be in search of warmer or cooler weather conditions, a greater

A. **Bar-tailed godwit** – This record-breaking bird makes the longest non-stop flight of any creature. It breeds in the Arctic before flying for nine days continuously to winter in Australia and New Zealand.

B. **Humpback whale** – This ocean giant makes the longest migration of any mammal: a 16,000 kilometre round trip from the warm waters of the tropics, where they reproduce,

to their feeding grounds at the Poles. Many other whales (including the largest species on Earth, the blue whale) migrate to the Poles in summer as the longer days and warmer waters provide more food.

C. **Arctic tern** – The longest recorded round trip of any migrating animal sees the Arctic tern travelling more than 70,000 kilometres in a single year, from the Arctic to

Antarctica, to take advantage of the summer at each Pole. During the course of its 30-year life, a single tern may travel more than 2.4 million kilometres!

D. **Wildebeest** – The annual migration of Africa's wildebeest from the Serengeti plains to the open grasslands of the Masai Mara involves more than a million individuals, making it one of the largest mass movements of any species.

E. **Globe skimmer dragonfly** – Holding the record for the longest insect migration, this dragonfly species will travel more than 15,000 kilometres. Following the rain, the dragon-flies leave the monsoons of India and travel to the rainy season in east- and southern-Africa – and return back again. No one single insect makes the whole journey. Instead, over four generations each play their part in this epic migratory relay race.

F. **Reindeer** – Travelling further than any other land-based mammal, over half a million reindeer journey more than 3,000 kilometres each year in search of food. Spending winter in the most southern part of their range, they return north for the brief summer bloom of plants across the Arctic tundra.

G. **Monarch butterfly** – More than 100 million monarch butterflies gather at the end

abundance of food, or better conditions in which to give birth and raise their young.

• Some creatures build reserves in preparation for their long journey by eating as much food as they can before they start, others continue to feed along the way. Migrating requires a lot of energy – some animals never make it to their journey's end.

• Migrating animals use different methods to find their way, responding to the magnetic field of the Earth, or the shape of land masses, even the mineral make-up of water can tell a migrating salmon how close it is to its destination.

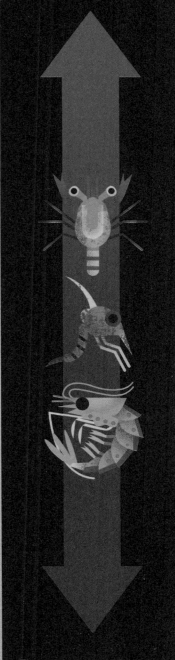

Despite their tiny size, some zooplankton swarms swim up and down through the ocean layers in a form of migration known as **diurnal vertical migration.**

of summer to sweep across North America to overwinter in Mexico. At 4,000 kilometres the migration cycle of this delicate insect is longer than its life cycle so no one butterfly makes the entire round trip.

H. **Red crab** – Once a year on Christmas Island in the Indian Ocean, the ground becomes a moving red carpet as more than 40 million crabs make their way from the forest to the sea in order to breed and lay their eggs. The whole red crab population moves together as the rainy season approaches, taking a week to make their 5 kilometre journey.

I. **Bluefin tuna** – A fast and powerful swimmer, the bluefin can reach speeds of up to 100 kilometres per hour and can dive to 1,000 metres. Like many other fish, it returns to its spawning grounds to breed and holds the record for one of the fastest migrations in the animal world. One tagged specimen travelled over 40,000 kilometres in just 20 months back and forth across the Pacific Ocean.

J. **King salmon** – Like most salmon, this fish returns to spawn in the very place it was born. The journey, often of more than 3,000 kilometres, will take it from its adult feeding grounds in the Pacific Ocean to the freshwater river of its birth, swimming upstream, jumping rapids and small waterfalls to reach its final destination.

K. **Green turtle** – Like other turtle species, this ocean wanderer has an incredible ability to navigate its way back to its birthplace. It will travel more than 2,500 kilometres across the oceans in order to lay its eggs in a burrow on the exact beach where it hatched.

These microscopic creatures may travel nearly a kilometre, sometimes daily, as they move from the ocean depths to surface waters in order to feed during the hours of darkness. It is the greatest migratory journey in the world in terms of the number of individual creatures involved.

At the North Pole is the **ARCTIC**

Dense, white fur for warmth and camouflage

Small ears reduce heat loss

LIFE AT THE ENDS

A

D

C

B

Wide, furry paws

AT THE EDGE OF THE ARCTIC ICE

THE POLAR REGIONS ARE SOME OF THE MOST INHOSPITABLE PLACES ON EARTH. Only animals and plants specially adapted to survive the sub-zero temperatures, months of darkness and hurricane-force winds can live here.

There are many ways in which animals have adapted to thrive in these harsh conditions. They often have a thick layer of fat beneath their skin and dense fur to help keep them warm, and small ears to prevent heat loss. Some creatures use the snow itself to keep warm and sheltered, making dens or burrows beneath its icy blanket. Others only visit the poles in the warmer parts of the year, migrating there to feed and breed when food is plentiful.

The Arctic lies in the far north and is made up of a frozen ocean surrounded by miles of windswept land know as tundra.
• It is warmer than the Antarctic but temperatures still reach -40°C during the long winter.
• Many animals migrate here to feed and breed during the milder summer when it is light all day. Flowers bloom across the tundra and in the sea a surge of plankton provides a huge food source for animals of all kinds.

A. **Polar bear** – This permanent resident of the Arctic is an excellent swimmer, spending more time in water than on land. It hunts seals by waiting at their blowholes.

B. **Lemming** – This creature is an important food source for many animals. In winter, it builds extensive networks of tunnels, which it rarely leaves.

C. **Harp seal** – This excellent swimmer can stay underwater for an hour, and keep holes in the ice which it returns to, to breathe.

D. **Arctic fox** – This fox's dense fur has two layers: a woolly under-layer to trap warm air, and a longer outer coat that turns white in winter.

E. **Arctic tern** – Like thousands of birds, the tern flocks to the Arctic in summer for the plentiful food. But then, having raised its chicks, it flies to the Antarctic – the longest journey of any bird – to take advantage of the summer there, too!

F. **Walrus** – The walrus uses its enormous tusks to haul itself out of the water, fight off predators, open breathing holes in the ice and rake the seabed for shellfish to eat.

G. **Tundra plants** – All polar plants, like saxifrages and cotton grass, lichens and mosses, have adapted to their habitat by being compact and wind-resistant. They are an important source of food for many creatures.

I

J

H

OF THE EARTH

Fat reserves beneath skin for insulation

E

D

G

E

F

IN ANTARTICA'S FROZEN SEA

In the far south lies the continent of **Antarctica**, which remains covered year-round in ice up to a mile thick.

• Surrounded by the world's stormiest seas, its average yearly temperature is -49°C.

• During winter it is permanently dark for months on end.

• It is also the driest, windiest place on the Earth with winds reaching over

300 kilometres per hour and only a few centimetres of rainfall each year.

• Almost all life here is in the sea, where a huge number of creatures have adapted to live successfully in the freezing cold waters.

H. **Blue whale** – The largest animal ever to have lived on Earth, the blue whale can reach lengths of up to 33 metres, yet it eats only the tiniest food. Each year the blue whale like

many others of its kind visit Antarctica to feed on krill and other plankton, sieving them from the water through horny plates in its mouth known as baleen.

I. **Penguins** – Many types of penguin can be found in and around the Antarctic continent. Their dense, oily feathers – as many as 30 to the square centimetre – cover a thick layer of down and another of blubber, making them incredibly resistant to cold.

J. **Leopard seal** – Living at the edge of the pack ice, this

seal is a fast swimmer and fierce predator. It attacks penguins but will also eat other, smaller seals, seabirds, fish and krill.

K. **Orca** – Unlike the baleen whales, orcas belong to the group of toothed whales and are voracious predators. They often come to Antarctica to hunt prey in groups and use echolocation to find their food.

L. **Krill** – Feeding on micro-plankton, shrimp-like krill are a staple food for many other creatures and a crucial part of the ocean food chain. They are

found all over the world, but are particularly plentiful during the warmer summer months in Antarctica.

M. **Elephant seal** – Named after the males' long nose, this seal was once hunted close to extinction for its oil. The blubber from one large male could yield over 200 litres of oil.

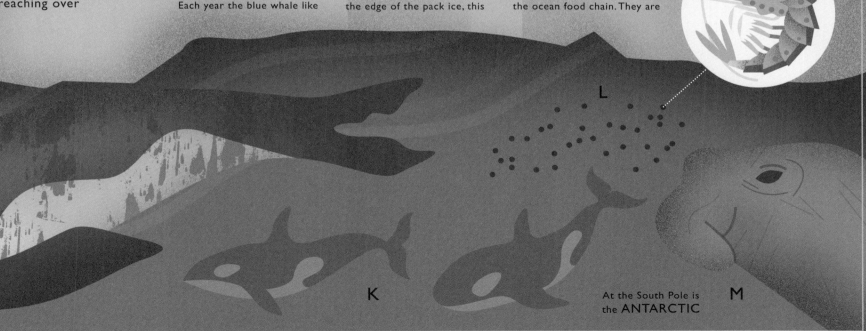

L

L

K

At the South Pole is the ANTARCTIC

M

33

SURPRISING PENGUINS

PENGUINS ARE A GROUP OF SEMI-ACQUATIC, FLIGHTLESS BIRDS. Today, there are 17 living species, all belonging to the order *Sphenisciformes*. Most inhabit the cold seas of the southern hemisphere, although a few live where cold sea currents flow into the tropics.

• Some extinct penguins were as tall as an adult human being.

• Penguins waddle along quite comically on land but spend half of their lives in the water. They are astonishingly agile, using their wings like flippers to swim after their food of fish and small marine animals.

• They have a thick coat of overlapping feathers that streamline their body, repel water and conserve heat, and a layer of fat called blubber to provide further insulation.

• To survive in extreme cold penguins have a special circulatory system, the **humeral arterial plexus**, that works as an efficient heat exchanger to conserve their body temperature.

A. **Emperor penguin** – During the Antarctic winter, colonies of this bird can number thousands. Once its single egg is laid, the female returns to the sea to feed. The male must survive without food for two months, protecting the egg from the extreme cold by carrying it on his feet under a 'pouch' of skin.

B. **King penguin** – Perfectly adapted to life in the water, it can dive up to 300 metres, swim at speeds of up to 10 kilometres per hour, and stay down for up to 20 minutes in pursuit of prey.

C. **Jackass penguin** – Found in warm waters around South Africa, the jackass penguin has pink glands above its eyes that work as a thermo-regulator to help it keep cool. It will also hold out its wings to release heat from its body.

D. **Adélie penguin** – Nesting colonies may number more than 200,000 birds when they gather in the summer to breed along the Antarctic shoreline.

E. **Chinstrap penguin** – As with many penguins, the chinstrap's markings help to camouflage it in the water. When seen from above, its dark back blends into the dark water; viewed from below its pale front blends into the light from above.

F. **Rockhopper penguin** – Like all crested penguins, the rockhopper has a plume of yellow feathers and a bulbous orange beak. Penguins use such features together with displays to help identify one another in their vast nesting colonies.

G. **Fairy penguin** – This extremely small species from Australia and New Zealand makes a burrow for its eggs in the ground or in a rocky crevice.

<table>
<tr><td colspan="2">PENGUIN SIZES</td></tr>
<tr><td>Emperor</td><td>– 1.3m</td></tr>
<tr><td>King</td><td>– 1m</td></tr>
<tr><td>Chinstrap</td><td>– 72cms</td></tr>
<tr><td>Jackass</td><td>– 70cms</td></tr>
<tr><td>Adélie</td><td>– 70cms</td></tr>
<tr><td>Rockhopper</td><td>– 50cms</td></tr>
<tr><td>Fairy</td><td>– 35cms</td></tr>
</table>

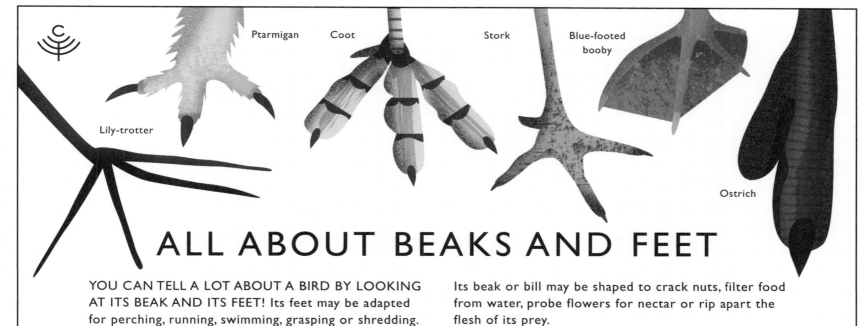

Ptarmigan Coot Stork Blue-footed booby

Lily-trotter

Ostrich

ALL ABOUT BEAKS AND FEET

YOU CAN TELL A LOT ABOUT A BIRD BY LOOKING AT ITS BEAK AND ITS FEET! Its feet may be adapted for perching, running, swimming, grasping or shredding.

Its beak or bill may be shaped to crack nuts, filter food from water, probe flowers for nectar or rip apart the flesh of its prey.

FEET

Finch – The single hind toe enables the bird to grasp a branch when perching.

Heron – Widely spread toes help prevent wading birds from sinking into the mud.

Mallard duck – Webbed feet help make ducks, geese and many seabirds efficient swimmers.

Rhea – Fewer toes help these flightless birds to run quickly and support their heavy bodies.

Woodpecker – Two toes to the front and to the back help a woodpecker climb easily in all directions.

Hawk – Long claws – well-adapted to catch and grasp prey – give many birds of prey difficulty walking.

BEAKS

Heron – This long and pointed beak is perfect for stabbing and grabbing fish.

Eagle – This sharp and hooked beak is useful for ripping and tearing flesh.

Duck – This broad and flat beak comes in handy when filtering water for food.

Parrot – This strong, hooked beak is good for cracking and shelling nuts.

Blackbird – This all-purpose beak is pointed for picking seeds or catching flies.

Woodpecker – This pointed, strong beak can chisel into the trunks of trees.

Pelican

Spoonbill

Flamingo

Toucan

Hummingbird

King vulture

Crossbill

Avocet

WHAT IS A BIRD?

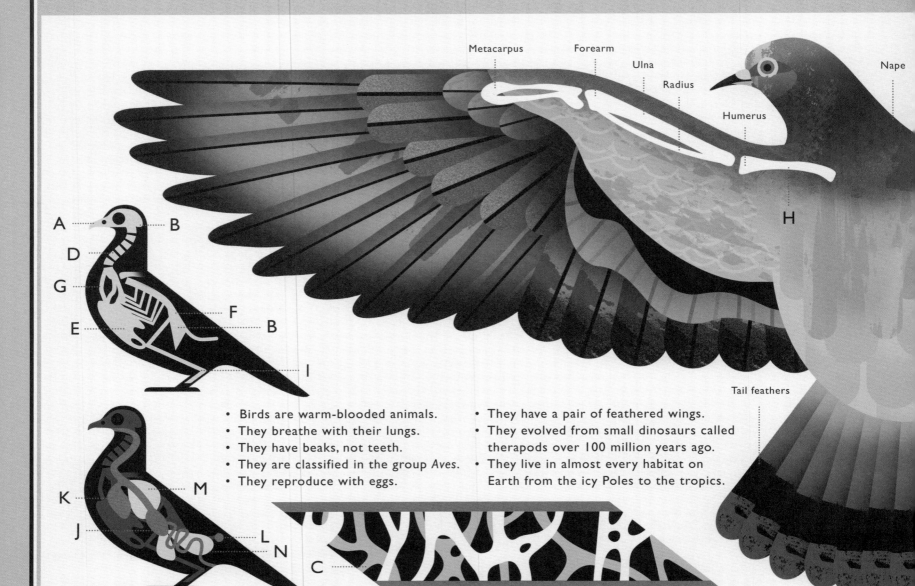

Metacarpus Forearm Ulna Radius Nape

Humerus

H

A — B
D
G
E — B
F
I

K — M
J — L N
C

- Birds are warm-blooded animals.
- They breathe with their lungs.
- They have beaks, not teeth.
- They are classified in the group *Aves*.
- They reproduce with eggs.

- They have a pair of feathered wings.
- They evolved from small dinosaurs called therapods over 100 million years ago.
- They live in almost every habitat on Earth from the icy Poles to the tropics.

Tail feathers

STRUCTURE OF A BIRD

BIRDS COME IN ALL SHAPES AND SIZES, from the world's smallest, the bee hummingbird, which weighs 1.6 grammes, to the African ostrich, which, at 125 kilogrammes, is our largest living bird and nearly 80,000 times heavier than its tiny relative! The basic structure of most flying birds is quite similar, though. Typically, they are a sleek and streamlined shape, which helps them to use as little energy as possible as they move through the air, and short, strong, compact bodies. Each has:

A. **Horny beak** – Much lighter than a mouthful of teeth!

B. **Fused bones** in its skull, pelvis and other parts of the body for extra strength.

C. **Honeycomb bones** – Many of a bird's major bones are hollow with a network of supportive internal struts. This helps to make a bird's skeleton lightweight but strong.

D. **Flexible neck** – Aids feeding, preening and all-round vision.

E. **Breastbone or keel** – A bird's powerful flight muscles attach to this. Overall, birds have 175 different muscles, and the pectoral muscles, which are used to flap the wings, are the largest.

F. **Pelvic girdle** – Strong and rigid for take-offs and landings.

G. **Wishbone** – A bird's collarbones are joined to keep its wing joints in position.

H. **Wing bones** – These are made up of the humerus, radius, ulna, forearm and metacarpus.

I. **False knee** – Although it may look as if a bird's knee is bending back to front, this is actually a bird's ankle. Its knee is at the top of its lower leg bone, hidden by its feathers.

J. **Gizzard** – Instead of teeth, this muscular bag is used to grind up food. A bird will swallow small stones, which also help.

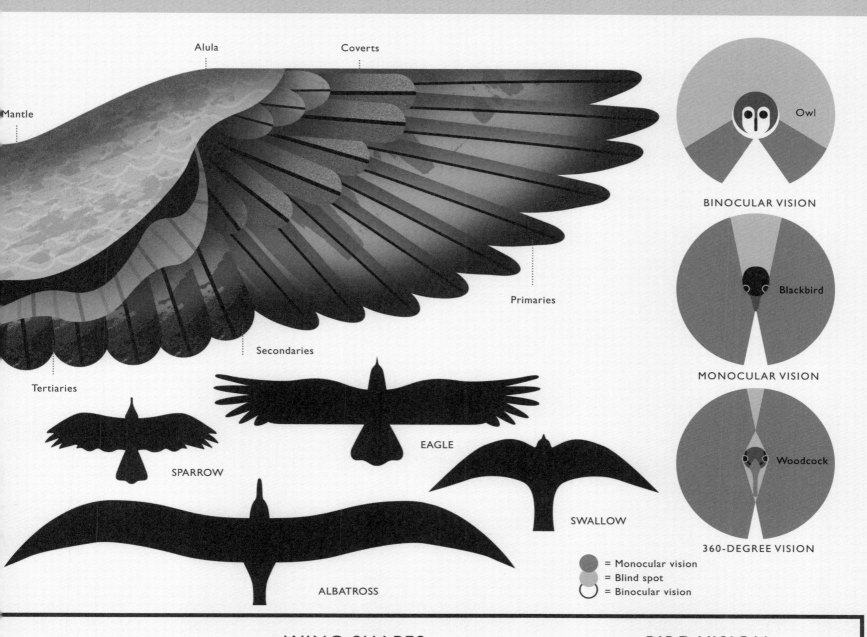

Mantle

Alula

Coverts

Primaries

Secondaries

Tertiaries

SPARROW

EAGLE

SWALLOW

ALBATROSS

Owl

BINOCULAR VISION

Blackbird

MONOCULAR VISION

Woodcock

360-DEGREE VISION

= Monocular vision
= Blind spot
= Binocular vision

WING SHAPES

K. **Crop** – A storage bag for food.
L. **Preen gland** – A bird covers its feathers with a waterproof oil that comes from here.
M. **Lungs** – A bird can take in lots of oxygen, which allows them to fly up high in the sky where oxygen is scarce.
N. **Air sacs** – These help to pump air through the respiratory system.

The shape of a bird's wings can tell you a lot about their style of flying.

Sparrow
The sparrow has short, rounded wings for quick take-off and good manoeuvrability in the air – useful if you're trying to escape a hungry hawk!

Eagle
Large soaring birds, like eagles and buzzards, have broad wings. Long flight feathers that splay out like fingers on a hand give them extra lift as they soar on upward air currents called thermals.

Swallow
Fast flyers like the swallow have pointed, backswept wings, which help them to swoop and dive at great speed while saving as much energy as possible.

Albatross
Gliding birds such as the albatross have long, narrow wings which allow them to soar and glide over the ocean for days – or weeks! – at a time.

BIRD VISION

Over time, the position of a bird's eyes has adapted to its lifestyle.

Binocular vision
Predatory birds, like owls, have eyes at the front of their heads. The view from each eye overlaps, giving the owl three-dimensional vision that helps it to track prey.

Monocular vision
Birds that are hunted, like blackbirds, have eyes nearer the sides of their heads. This gives better all-round view but less binocular sight.

360-degree vision
With eyes even further round the sides, woodcocks can see behind their heads!

ALL ABOUT FEATHERS

FEATHERS SET BIRDS APART FROM ALL OTHER LIVING ANIMALS. There are two basic kinds of feather: outer flight or contour feathers which give the bird its shape, and down feathers which form a layer that helps to keep the bird warm.

FEATHERS HAVE FIVE MAIN FUNCTIONS:
1. They allow the bird to fly.
2. They keep the bird warm.
3. Some species can coat their feathers with a waterproof oil.
4. They can provide camouflage.
5. They are used for display.

STRUCTURE OF A FEATHER
A flight feather needs to form an unbroken surface for air to flow over the top of. To help create this continous plane, a feather has barbs that mesh together, hooking onto their neighbours on either side thanks to minute side branches called barbules. If the feathers get ruffled, a bird simply runs its beak along the feather to zip the barbs back into place again. This is called **preening**.

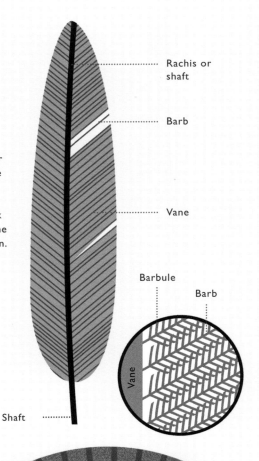

Rachis or shaft

Barb

Vane

Barbule

Barb

Vane

Shaft

TYPES OF FEATHER
A. Vaned flight feather
B. Contour or body feather
C. Tail feather
D. Down feather
E. Semi-plume
F. Filoplume
G. Bristle feather

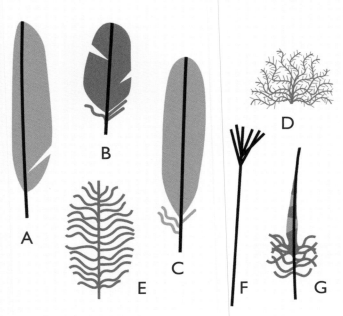

A

B

C

D

E

F

G

THE MATING GAME

Some birds have amazing headdresses, called **plumes**, made up of oddly shaped feathers. It is often the males that have these fine crests and crowns which they use to great effect in the breeding season in an attempt to attract a mate, but in some species they can also help birds to identify one another.

COCK-OF-THE-ROCK

ROCKHOPPER PENGUIN

CROWNED CRANE

KEY TO SPECIES
A. **Macaw** (flight)
B. **Pheasant** (tail)
C. **King-of-saxony bird of paradise** (head)
D. **Buzzard** (flight)
E. **Peacock** (tail)
F. **Emu** (wing)
G. **Standard-winged nightjar** (tail)
H. **Flamingo** (body)
I. **Satyr tragopan** (tail)
J. **Egret** (plume)
K. **Mandarin duck** (head)
L. **Guineafowl** (body)
M. **Jay** (wing)

Birds' feathers come in a remarkable array of colours and patterns. Head and tail feathers in some species are often strikingly coloured to aid in courtship displays.

HOW TO HIDE

CAMOUFLAGE IS A SURVIVAL TACTIC USED BY MANY ANIMAL GROUPS. Being coloured, patterned or shaped to blend in with your background is such a successful technique

CRYPTIC COLOURS

The eggs and chicks of ground-nesting birds such as this sandpiper are often **cryptically coloured**, so closely matching the colour and pattern of their background that they can remain unseen by predators. The adult birds often are a completely different colour from their young as they do not need the same measure of protection.

STANDING STILL

Many camouflaged creatures are also experts at keeping still! In addition to its wonderfully camouflaged plumage this bittern will remain immobile if danger threatens, often pointing its head to the sky, helping it to look even more like part of the reed bed in which it hides.

By herding together, these zebras use something called **motion dazzle** to further confuse predators. The mass of contrasting stripes makes it hard to pick out a single animal to attack, giving the zebras an improved chance of escape.

The irregular pattern on the coat of a tiger is an example of **disruptive colouration**. The pattern of light and dark confuses the eye so the animal's outline is hard to see, which is useful when stalking prey or hiding from enemies.

that it can effectively make a creature 'disappear'. This can be used not only to help animals hide from predators, but also to help predators creep up unseen on their unsuspecting prey.

Some kinds of camouflage work most successfully when creatures are grouped together, such as the zebras seen below. Others are employed on individual creatures.

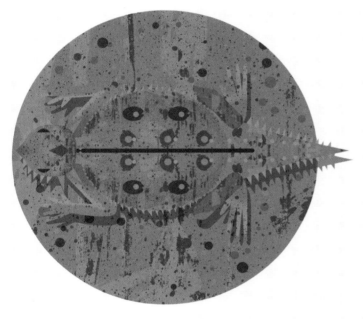

SHADOW-DODGING
In the desert your shadow can give you away no matter how well-coloured you are to match your surroundings. The flat-tailed horned lizard overcomes this by pressing its body to the ground. A fringe of scales along its sides helps to eliminate any shadows cast by the sun, thereby making it incredibly hard to spot.

A CHANGE OF COLOUR
Various species of reptile, fish, frog, squid and octopus can actively change their skin patterns and colours to resemble their current background. Over a longer period, animals such as the Arctic fox can change the colour of its fur by moulting, becoming white in winter to match its snowy habitat.

CHART No.18

Focus on Nature:
CHAMELEON – MASTER OF COLOUR

MASTERS OF COLOUR CHANGE, CHAMELEONS ARE ALSO THE SHARP-SHOOTERS OF THE ANIMAL WORLD. They can flick their tongues further than their body length to catch their prey.

• Most species change colour as a visual signal – to warn off rivals or attract mates, or to show anger or fear. It can also help control its body temperature, becoming lighter when it needs to lose body heat and vice versa.

• To disguise itself, the horned leaf chameleon has skin flaps that make it look like a leaf and it will even sway from side to side on a branch, mimicking a leaf blowing in the wind.

• Most chameleons eat insect prey but larger ones will eat small mammals and one species – Meller's chameleon – feeds mainly on small birds.

• Like other reptiles, most chameleons lay eggs, but some, such as Jackson's, give birth to live young.

Jackson's chameleon has three prominent head horns, used by the males for display and fighting rivals.

• The chameleon's amazing tongue can travel at speeds of over 5 metres per second, reaching its prey in less than one-hundredth of a second. The tip of its tongue is covered in sticky mucus to help it keep hold of its catch.

• A chameleon can change the colour and pattern of its skin from being near-white to having brilliant stripes. It does this by expanding or contracting pigment cells in its skin called **chromatophores**.

• The chameleon has large eyes covered by skin so that only the pupil is visible. They can swivel their eyes independently in any direction for complete 360° vision – excellent for spotting prey.

• Is has a **prehensile** tail that can be used to grip branches like a fifth limb.

• The Chameleon is the only other creature apart from a bird to have **zygodactylous** feet, tong-like in appearance with toes pointing front and back, giving them expert grasping and climbing ability.

WHAT IS A REPTILE?

REPTILES HAVE LIVED ON EARTH FOR MORE THAN 300 MILLION YEARS. Today, there are more than 10,000 species of these mostly egg-laying vertebrates, belonging to the class *Reptilia*.

• Reptiles are most common in warm regions because they are **ectothermic** which means that most of their body heat is drawn from their surroundings, not produced by themselves. They must rely on their environment and behaviour to keep their body temperature stable, basking in the sun to warm up, or sheltering from it when they need to cool down.

• Reptiles vary enormously in size and shape but all have tough skin with a covering of scales made, like human hair and fingernails, from a horny substance called **keratin**. They shed these scales periodically in order to grow.

• Most reptiles lay their eggs on land, even those that spend their lives mainly in water. The eggs hatch into miniature versions of their parents rather than going through a larval stage like many species of amphibians.

A. Tortoises and turtles – These hard-shelled reptiles have existed for almost 200 million years when similar looking creatures walked side by side with the dinosaurs. Tortoises live on land, turtles in the water, but both have a distinctive shell for protection and camouflage. Some species can live for over 100 years and grow up to 2 metres in length. Others travel thousands of miles in search of food or to reach their nesting sites where they bury their eggs in specially-dug chambers.

B. Crocodilians – This order includes the crocodiles and alligators. Most live in or near water and all are fierce predators. They have evolved a highly successful hunting technique, laying in wait at the water's edge with only their eyes and nostrils showing, ready to ambush any creature which comes in range. Their skin is covered in bony, plate-like scales, camouflaged in shades of brown, grey and black. They lay their eggs near water, either in the ground or under rotting vegetation.

C. Lizards – More than half of all living reptiles are lizards. They tend to live where it is warm, are adept at running, climbing and burrowing thanks to their well-developed limbs and long tails, and are covered in a huge variety of scales in all shapes, sizes, colours and patterns. Lizards have evolved many defence strategies, from the use of camouflage to those that have a poisonous bite or protective spines. Incredibly, many species can also shed their tail if attacked and later grow a new one!

D. Tuatara – Similar in appearance to lizards, the tuatara is the last survivor of the prehistoric beak-headed reptiles. Found only on remote islands off the coast of New Zealand, tuataras live in burrows and come out only at night to feed on insects. They grow incredibly slowly, and do not breed until the females are at least 20 years old. Their soft, leathery eggs, once laid, may take up to a year to hatch but it is thought that individuals can then live for up to 100 years.

E. Snakes – Formidable and highly evolved predators, snakes have no limbs, no eyelids and no external ears. They can move easily, swimming in water and climbing up trees thanks to their highly flexible skeleton. They kill their prey either by biting or through constriction. Thanks to their flexible jaws, and highly elastic skin, snakes can swallow whole creatures much larger than themselves. Many snakes are highly venomous, injecting their venom through modified teeth called fangs.

DESERT LIFE

DESERTS MAY BE SHORT ON WATER, BUT THEY'RE NOT SHORT ON WILDLIFE. The only way to survive in this extreme climate is through evolutionary adaptation and many creatures have successfully done just that.
• Africa's Sahara Desert is the single largest hot desert on Earth – at over 9 million square kilometres.
• In summer the daytime temperature can soar to 47°C, often for several months at a time. There is less than 10 centimetres of rain per year, even less in the central areas, and hurricane force winds often cause punishing sandstorms and dust devils (a type of whirlwind).
• The wildlife that lives here has adapted to these hyper-arid conditions in a variety of ways. In the heart of the desert, most mammals are relatively small to help minimise water loss and often meet their need for water just from eating food. Some may never drink water in their entire lives. Many take refuge in burrows during the heat of the day and forage at night when it is cooler. Others have physical adaptations to help them cope with this harshest of climates.

A

B

Slit nostrils can be closed as protection from sandstorms

Thick eyelashes keep out the sand and sun

Leathery mouth for feeding on thorny desert plants

Muscular legs for long-distance walking

Wide, twin-toed feet help prevent the animal from sinking into the sand

A. **Dromedary camel** – An expert at water storage, this camel can drink over 50 litres in just a few minutes, and then go for days without drinking at all. Contrary to popular belief, its hump is used for storing fat, not water, which enables it to go for long periods without eating, and its particularly long large intestine helps absorb every last bit of water and nutrient from its food.

B. **Fennec fox** – With a sandy-coloured coat that blends in with its desert background, this hunter looks for small mammals, birds and insects. Its large ears help it to lose body heat and allow it to hear prey beneath the ground. Fur on the base of its feet protects it when walking over the burning hot sand.

C. **Addax** – Also known as the screwhorn antelope, this animal can survive without drinking water for long periods, instead getting moisture from its food and from the dew that condenses on desert plants. It expertly tracks rainfall and will journey across the desert in search of plants that spring up quickly whenever rain falls. Its pale coat reflects the sun's rays, helping it to keep cool, and its oversized hooves make it adept at walking on the desert sands.

D. **Desert jerboa** – This rodent – related to rats and squirrels – comes out only at night from its burrow beneath the sand. It rarely drinks water, extracting moisture from its diet of desert plants and insects.

E. **Sandfish lizard** – This type of skink 'swims' through sand to escape the heat – and other predators! It has shiny scales, fringed feet for burrowing and tiny nostrils to keep sand out of its nose and lungs.

F. **Horned viper** – This snake burys itself in the sand to catch passing prey, where its patterned scales blends in perfectly with its background. It can travel fast over loose sand by weaving its body from side to side, a form of locomotion known as sidewinding, which leaves a distinctively patterned track in its wake.

G. **Desert scarab beetle** – This species of dung beetle gets all of food and water from the dung it collects. Pairs of beetles will roll and bury a ball of dung as a food store and in which they lay their eggs.

H. **Date palms, tamarisks** and **acacias** – There are few plants in the heart of the desert, but where there are springs, an oasis – or wadi – will form. Here, specialised trees and shrubs will grow, their long roots reaching down to reach precious water far below the desert sands. When rain does fall, the seeds of flowering plants sprout very quickly, completing their growth cycle and producing new seeds in a matter of days before the soil dries out again.

THE MIGHTY SAGUARO

TOWERING ABOVE NORTH AMERICA'S SONORAN DESERT, THE SAGUARO IS ONE OF THE WORLD'S TALLEST CACTI. Perfectly adapted to life in this hot, dry climate, it is the centre of a community, providing food and shelter to a host of other desert dwellers.

• The saguaro has sharp spines instead of leaves and a waxy skin to reduce water loss. Pleats in the skin surface expand to hold and store moisture whenever rain does fall, and the wide, shallow root system ensures maximum absorbtion of water from the surrounding soil.

• Saguaros can reach over 15 metres in height. An adult plant may live for 150 years and be over 2 tonnes in weight.

• Despite its prickly appearance, many birds and insects live amongst its sharp spines. Gila woodpeckers hollow out nests from its fleshy trunk, which are adopted in turn by elf owls.

• In the spring, strong-smelling flowers attract birds, bats and insects in search of pollen and nectar. Each flower blooms for only one day.

• Once pollinated, the flowers produce bright red fruits, packed full of seeds. These provide a vital source of food to many desert animals, such as jackrabbits, coyotes and peccaries. In return, they disperse the seeds to other parts of the desert, allowing new saguaros to grow.

• When the saguaro finally dies, its rotting flesh provides another rich source of water and nutrients for many desert insects.

DETAIL OF SPINES

RED-TAILED HAWK

COSTA'S HUMMINGBIRD

GILA WOODPECKER

ELF OWL

MEXICAN LONG-TONGUED BAT

COYOTE

HAWK NEST

SAP BEETLE

PECCARY

WASP NEST

JACK-RABBIT

DESERT TORTOISE

PRICKLY PEAR CACTUS

BARREL CACTUS

SUPER SPINES

MANY CREATURES, BOTH VERTEBRATE AND INVERTEBRATE, HAVE BODIES COVERED WITH SHARP SPINES. These are most often found on prey animals and are used as a highly effective form of protection. In spiny mammals, the spines are modified hairs with a soft centre covered in a hard layer of keratin (the same material that forms human fingernails and hair). In insects, crustaceans and other invertebrates, the spines form part of the creature's exoskeleton. In some species, the spines are capable of injecting venom – a double-defence against attack by predators.

The **echidna**, or spiny anteater, of New Guinea and Australia has a round body covered in fur and as many as 500 sharp spines. When threatened, it will curl into a ball or wedge itself in a crevice or hole using its spines as a defensive shield. Its short, strong front legs and large claws allow it to hold fast against any predator trying to remove it. One of only five living species of mammals that lay eggs, called **monotremes**, the echidna has a tiny mouth and a long, sticky tongue. It feeds by tearing open rotten logs and anthills to collect its food of earthworms and ants.

Porcupine fish – This spiny fish will gulp water when threatened, puffing up its body into a spiky ball. This makes it hard for the fish to swim – but even harder to attack!

Sea urchin – Most species of urchin are covered in hard, brittle spines. Some have spines that secrete a poisonous substance that can cause severe irritation to predators who brush against them. The spines can also be used to help wedge the urchin into crevices in rocks and reefs.

Thorny devil lizard – This lizard's armoury of sharp spines across its whole body protect it whilst feeding. Unlike most lizards, it spends a lot of time foraging in one place on the ground where it is vulnerable to attack. It hunts for ants and can consume thousands during a single meal.

Rice hispa beetle – Although tiny, at only 7 millimetres long, this is a dangerous pest which, along with its larvae, decimates rice crops in Southeast Asia by eating the leaves. Its flat body is covered by short, sharp spines which helps protect it from attack by predators.

BEWILDERING BEETLES

ONE OUT OF EVERY FOUR LIVING ANIMAL SPECIES ON EARTH IS A BEETLE. With nearly 400,000 known species, beetles make up one third of all insects, from the giant American longhorn (the length of a human hand) to the tiny feather-winged beetle that would fit on a pinhead.

• All beetles belong to the order *Coleoptera* and the first ones appeared nearly 300 million years ago.

• Unlike other flying insects, beetles have hard forewings, called **elytra**, which close like a protective case over their backs. These are often brightly coloured or patterned, and some have an iridescent or metallic sheen.

• Beetles start life as larvae and metamorphose into their adult form.

• They live in virtually all types of habitat, including underwater, and between them, beetles consume a wide variety of foods – eating rotten wood, dung and the remains of dead animals, as well as pollen, leaves, insects and other invertebrates.

• Over millions of years beetles have developed a bewildering array of survival strategies. Some are equipped with fearsome antlers to frighten or fight rivals or have hairy bodies to irritate the mouths of predators, or cases covered in spikes to prevent attack. Many are experts at camouflage and some are shaped to mimic inanimate objects such as leaves or bark. Others resemble their stinging relatives, the bees and ants, or advertise a horrid taste through warning colours on their wing cases.

• Many beetles were prominent in ancient cultures, most notably the sacred scarab, a type of dung beetle, which was worshipped by the Ancient Egyptians.

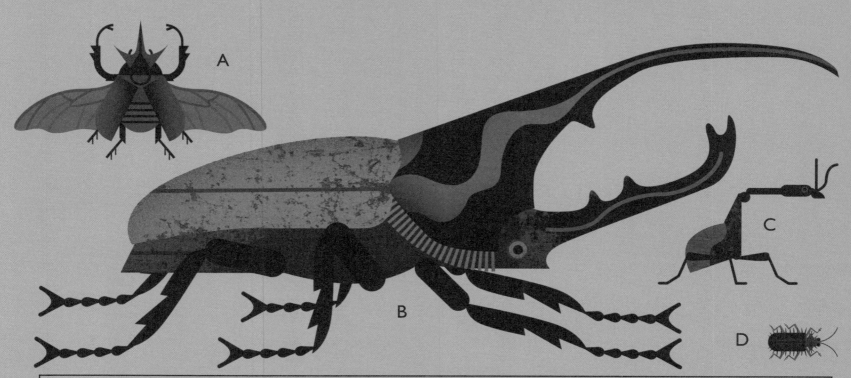

KEY TO SPECIES WITH APPROXIMATE SIZES				
A. **Rhinoceros beetle** 22-60mm	D. **Rice hispa beetle** 7mm	H. **Tortoise beetle** 13mm	L. **Schoenherr's weevil** 21-23mm	P. **Scarab dung beetle** 5-30mm
B. **Hercules beetle** 170mm	E. **Wallace's jewel beetle** – 40-60mm	I. **Tiger beetle** 10-24mm	M. **Goliath beetle** 60-250mm	Q. **Seven-spot ladybird** 7-10mm
C. **Giraffe weevil** 250mm	F. **Bee beetle** 9-12mm	J. **Great diving beetle** 27-35mm	N. **Pennsylvania firefly** 10-15mm	R. **Harlequin beetle** 30-78mm
	G. **Colorado potato beetle** – 10mm	K. **Madagascan click beetle** 23-25mm	O. **Javan violin beetle** 60-90mm	

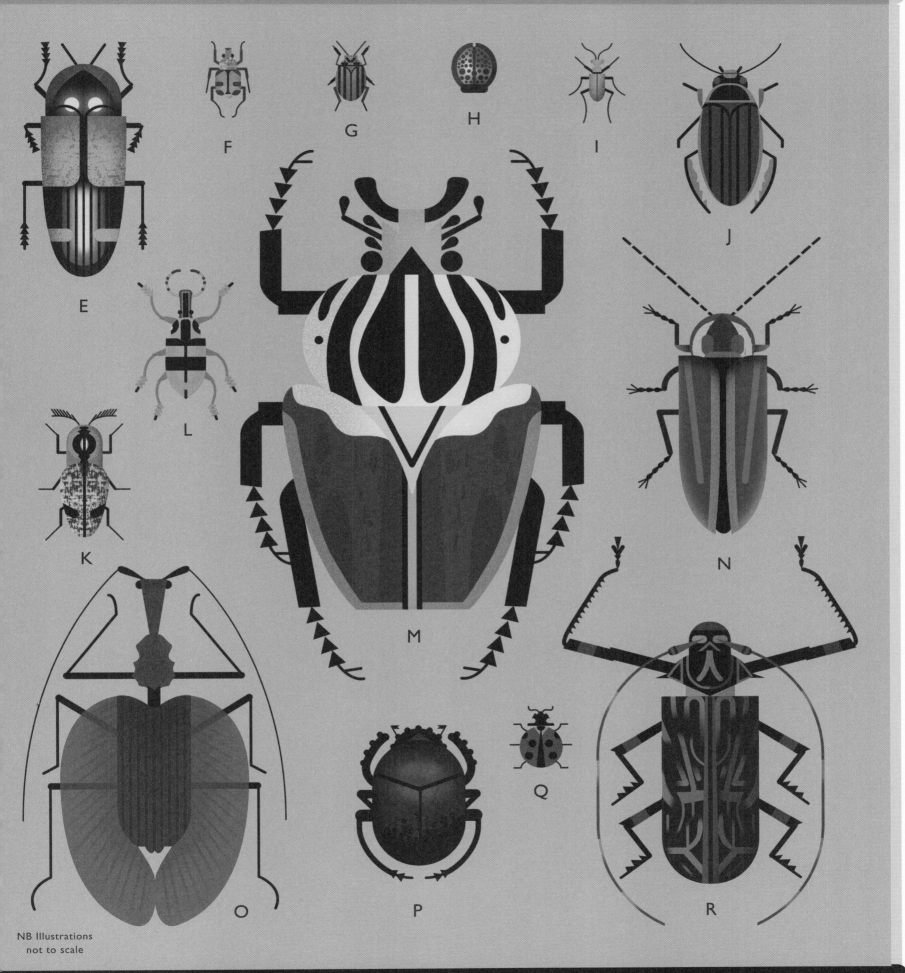

E

F

G

H

I

J

K

L

M

N

O

P

Q

R

NB Illustrations
not to scale

Journey through Nature:

LIFE IN TROPICAL RAINFORESTS

RAINFORESTS ARE OFTEN CALLED THE LUNGS OF OUR PLANET. They stretch like a great green ocean over thousands of square miles around the equator and their lush vegetation absorbs huge amounts of carbon dioxide, a greenhouse gas, and produces oxygen upon which we depend for survival. As well as helping to stabilise our climate, rainforests also provide a home for over half of all the plants and animal species on Earth but, although we know most of the bird and animal species that live there, scientists believe there are many more plants and invertebrates still to be discovered.

Rainforests are divided into layers according to the plants that grow there: the emergent layer, the canopy, the understory and the forest floor. Below, you can see just a small selection of the many species that live in some of our oldest rainforests, on the tropical islands of Southast Asia. Turn the page to find out more about the amazing diversity of life in this important habitat.

EMERGENT

Orchid

Fungi

WHO LIVES HERE?

THE RAINFORESTS OF SOUTHEAST ASIA ABOUND WITH AN AMAZING DIVERSITY OF LIFE, from the top of the trees to the shady forest floor tens of metres below.

Some creatures remain high in the canopy all their lives, never descending to the ground, and are specially adapted to make the most of their high-rise life.

FOREST LAYERS

• The highest layer of the rainforest – up to 75 metres above the forest floor – is made up of giant trees called **emergents**. Many have trunks with massive buttresses for support. Plentiful sunlight is enjoyed by monkeys, bats, butterflies and eagles.

• Beneath is the **canopy** which grows to 30 metres: a dense layer of foliage which forms a roof over the forest below. The maze of leaves and branches provides food and shelter for most of the forest's animal life.

• Little sunlight reaches the **understory** layer beneath, and few of the trees grow more than a few metres high. Insects abound here, as well as many other animals including leopards, tree frogs and nocturnal hunters such as the slow loris.

• The final layer is the **forest floor** where there is little light. Fungi abound, and the leaf litter provides food for many small creatures.

• **Epiphytes**, plants that grow on other plants, such as orchids, ferns and lianas are found at most levels.

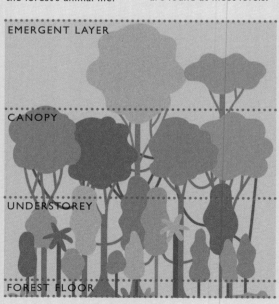

EMERGENT LAYER

CANOPY

UNDERSTOREY

FOREST FLOOR

A. **Grey langur** – Roosts high in the trees at night and descends by day to eat.

B. **Monkey-eating eagle** – This rare eagle is found in the Philippines.

C. **Birdwing butterfly** – Named for its exceptional size and bird-like flight.

D. **Silvery gibbon** – This territorial monkey rarely descends to the ground.

E. **Flying fox** – Also called a fruit bat, this is the largest bat in the world.

F. **Fire-tufted barbet** – This bird eats fruits and scatters seeds in its droppings.

G. **Colugo** – A membrane of skin between this flying lemur's limbs helps it glide.

H. **Atlas moth** – This is one of the world's largest moths. Males can smell a mate from many kilometres.

I. **Proboscis monkey** – This monkey is named for its large, fleshy nose, which swells when it is angry.

J. **Hornbill** – This bird collects fruit from high branches with its long bill.

K. **Orangutan** – This tree-dwelling ape's name means 'person of the forest' in Malay.

L. **Dawn bat** – This important pollinator probes forest flowers with its long tongue in search of nectar.

M. **White-lipped pit viper** – This venomous snake eats birds, frogs and small mammals.

N. **Rück's blue flycatcher** – This species is found only on the island of Sumatra.

O. **Blue-streaked lory** – This parrot has a brush-tipped tongue evolved for its diet of fruit and nectar.

P. **Javan gliding frog** – This frog's webbed feet help it glide from branch to branch.

Q. **Slow loris** – This slow-moving nocturnal hunter feeds on insects.

R. **Walking stick** – This perfectly camouflaged stick insect can reach over 30 centimetres in length.

S. **Spotted civet** – The spotted coat of this

graceful hunter helps conceal it from its prey of small mammals.

T. **Lotus mantis** – This insect mimics a flower to ambush its prey.

U. **Leopard** – This adept climber drags prey up into the trees where it can eat undisturbed.

V. **Sun bear** – The 'honey bear' is so-called for its love of honeycomb and honey.

W. **Leech** – This distant relative of the earthworms sucks blood from its prey.

X. **Babirusa** – The distinctive upper canine teeth of the male babirusa grow upwards through its muzzle and can reach 30 centimetres in length.

Y. **Tailorbird** – This species gets its name from the way it builds its nest, using its beaks to 'sew' together leaves with plant fibres or spider silk.

Z. **Rhinoceros beetle** – This beetle hides during the day and comes out at night to feed on plant sap.

Focus on Nature:
THE CURIOUS AYE-AYE

THE AYE-AYE IS ONE OF THE WORLD'S RAREST CREATURES.
• It is a type of lemur, which sleeps, eats, travels and mates in the dense foliage of the rainforest and comes out only at night.
• It uses echolocation to find food, tapping at tree trunks and listening for sounds of insect larvae wriggling beneath the bark.
• It gnaws a hole and uses its long fourth finger to dig out grubs.

• It makes a nest of sticks and leaves in which to raise its young. The nests are shared in succession by other aye-ayes.
• Its offspring stay with their parents for two years.
• Once believed extinct, the aye-aye is threatened in the wild due to destruction of its habitat.
• In Malagasy legend the aye-aye was a symbol of death.

Large eyes help the aye-aye to see in the dark

Huge bat-like ears can hear wood-boring grubs under bark

Ridges on inner surface of ear help focus sound

Cat-sized body covered in shaggy fur

Powerful back legs help the aye-aye to leap from tree to tree like a squirrel

Rodent-like, ever-growing teeth for gnawing bark

Thin third finger for tapping and grooming

Long fourth finger with double-jointed tip to dig out grubs

Habitat: Madagascan rainforest
Size: 40 centimetre body; 40 centimetre tail
Weight: 3 kilogrammes
Diet: Insects, fruit, seeds, fungi, birds' eggs

BRILLIANT BATS

Bats are the only mammals that can truly fly and most of them are nocturnal. To avoid flying into things and to find their food in the dark, most insect-eating bats use **echolocation**, sending out bursts of high-frequency sound waves using their mouth or nose.

• When the sound bounces off an object, it sends back an echo. The bat can then identify an object by the 'sound shape' of the echo that returns.

• Large, mobile ears help bats to pick up sound and also the vibrations of an insect's wings.

• Once a bat has located its prey, it will scoop it up in mid-air, often using its thumb claw to put food in its mouth.

• During the day, nocturnal bats will roost in buildings, caves or hollow trees, hanging upside down from their clawed feet.

The **olm**, a type of salamander, has adapted to a life of almost complete darkness. It inhabits underground streams in caves in Central and Southern Europe, has a pinkish skin almost devoid of pigment and only rudimentary eyes. It hunts its prey of small invertebrates using its acute sense of smell and hearing.

The folds of skin on the nose of the **horseshoe bat** focus its squeaks into narrow beams of sound. It will sweep its head from side to side to scan for insects whilst flying through the darkness.

The **star-nosed mole** spends almost its entire life underground. Instead of using its tiny eyes, it relies on the extremely sensitive tentacles, called rays, at the end of its snout to feel for food.

LIVING IN THE DARK

AS NIGHT FALLS, MANY ANIMALS THAT SLEEP OR REST BY DAY EMERGE FROM THEIR HIDING PLACES TO HUNT AND FEED. These **nocturnal** creatures have evolved to make the most of a lifestyle that avoids competition for food and other resources with animals that are active during the day. It may also help them to avoid predators, or the burning daytime sun of a hot desert. Nocturnal animals have many adaptations to help them navigate, avoid predators, find food and attract mates in the dark.

Night-hunting owls use their extraordinary hearing to help them pinpoint prey rustling in the grass. Their ears are at slightly different heights, which gives them directional hearing.

The **aye-aye** uses many senses to help it hunt for food in the darkness of the rainforest – its huge eyes, enormous ears and its ability to use echo-location are all valuable tools for a night-time raid.

Snakes do not have to rely on just their eyesight to detect prey – they can 'taste' the air using their tongues to detect the presence of food. Certain types of snake also have an additional sense to help them – a heat-sensitive pit on each side of their head that can detect infrared radiation. Even in total darkness the snake can sense the heat given off by its prey and strike with deadly accuracy.

The feathery antennae of many male **moths** can detect attractive smelling chemicals, called **pheromones**, released by the females. This enables them to locate a mate in the darkness.

EYES IN THE DARKNESS

Many nocturnal animals have large eyes in relation to the size of their bodies. The larger the eye, the more efficient it is at gathering light, helping its owner see better in the dusk or dark. The shape of the pupil can also help – vertically slit pupils, like those of cats and nocturnal snakes, can open widely to allow the maximum amount of light to enter the eye.

Many nocturnal animals also have a special mirror-like layer at the back of their eye, called the **tapetum lucidum**, which reflects light and makes the eye more sensitive to low light. It is the reason why some animals' eyes appear to shine in the dark when light hits them.

The **gecko's** pupil can open wide to receive maximum light at night but closes to a series of pinholes to block out bright sunlight during the daylight hours.

A. **Bushbaby**
B. **Cat**
C. **Nocturnal snake**
D. **Gecko**

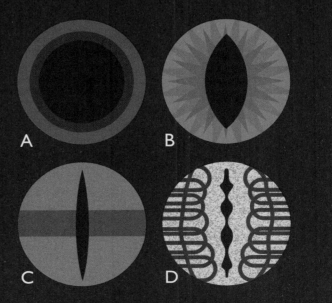

SUPER-POWERED OWLS

TAWNY OWL

Flat face with circle of feathers around eyes that can be adjusted to focus sound towards ears

Large forward-facing eyes give binocular vision

Short, hooked bill for gripping and tearing food

Dull coloured plumage and patterning for camouflage

Powerful, feathered feet

Sharp talons for catching and crushing prey

OWLS ARE SUPERBLY ADAPTED AS NIGHT-FLYING PREDATORS.

• Their large eyes gather all the available light and face forwards, giving them the greatest area of binocular vision.

• They cannot swivel their eyes to see from side to side. Instead, they can rotate their heads more than 270 degrees for a nearly all-round view.

• They have acute hearing, with forward-facing earholes set at different levels to help the owl pinpoint sounds. This is called **binaural** or **directional** hearing.

• Soft plumage enables owls to fly almost silently so they can hear the faintest rustle of prey below, in grass or even under snow.

• Most owls feed on insects, birds or small mammals. Some have adapted to catch fish.

• Owls generally swallow their prey whole. After several hours they regurgitate the indigestible parts as a pellet.

• Owls nest in cavities – in trees, on the ground or in crevices in rocks or buildings.

• Owl eggs are usually white and almost round in shape, which is typical of eggs that are laid in hidden places.

• There are around 200 living species of owl, of the order *Strigiformes*. They are found in every habitat, from dense forest to Arctic tundra.

• Owls are one of the oldest known groups of landbirds, dating from 60 million years ago.

Flight feather

Owl pellet

GREAT HORNED OWL

Fringed, soft-edged wing feathers for near-silent flight

BARN OWL

SNOWY OWL

ELF OWL

WHO'S IN THE TREE?

IN GENERAL, THE OLDER A TREE, THE MORE LIFE IT SUPPORTS. This ancient oak may have lived for nearly 600 years and within its spreading branches it provides food and shelter for many types of creature. In spring its young leaves are food for insect larvae – one tree could provide food for hundreds of thousands of caterpillars alone whilst in autumn its acorns are eaten by insects, birds and small mammals. All year round creatures burrow beneath its bark, nest amongst its branches or thrive in the deep litter made by its falling leaves. And when night falls a new cast of characters emerges – owls, bats, badgers and mice – who have sheltered amongst its roots or in hollows within its trunk during the hours of daylight.

Sparrowhawk

Purple hairstreak butterfly and caterpillar

Pipistrelle bats

Oak gall wasp and gall

Oak bark beetle

Green tortrix moth and caterpillar

Acorn

Tawny owl

Centipede

Great spotted woodpecker

Tawny owl chicks

Eyed hawkmoth

Red fox

Badger

Grey squirrel

Ivy

Wood mice

Dryad's saddle fungus

THE SECRET LIFE OF PLANTS

WITHOUT PLANTS THERE WOULD BE NO LIFE ON OUR PLANET. Every food chain on Earth starts with a plant, yet plants cannot move about to find food as animals do. Instead they have to make their own, through a process called **photosynthesis**. This uses light energy from the sun to make food for the plant and ultimately for every creature on the planet. Through this same process plants also produce most of the oxygen that we need to breathe, so next time you look at a plant, remember – it may not look as if it is doing very much but in fact it is quietly doing two of the most important jobs of all living things.

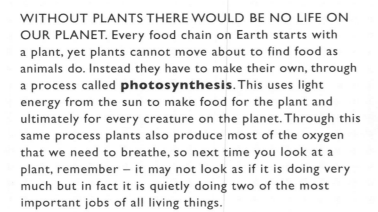

A

B

C

D

E

F

GERMINATION

An acorn falls to the earth, warmed by the sun, watered by the rain. With these two things it has all it needs to fulfil its purpose – to grow into a new plant. If conditions are favourable, the acorn will send out a root, then a shoot, eventually growing into an oak tree that will produce acorns of its own.

  Over time a whole forest could grow from just this one tiny acorn, providing food and shelter for many different creatures.

A. **Acorn cup**
B. **Fruit wall** – the outer surface of the nut.
C. **Seed coat** – called the **testa**, this is a hard outer case that protects the softer centre.

D. **Cotyledons** – these will grow into the plant's embryonic (initial) leaves.
E. **Plumule** – this will grow into the plant's first shoot.
F. **Radicle** – this will grow into the plant's first root.

Together, the radicle, plumule and cotyledons form the **embryo**.

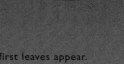

Sensing warmth and moisture, the acorn casing splits and a tiny root appears.

The root grows downwards towards the earth and takes in water from the soil.

A green shoot appears and grows upwards, towards the light.

The first leaves appear. Now the plant is ready to start making its own food through photosynthesis.

HOW PHOTOSYNTHESIS WORKS

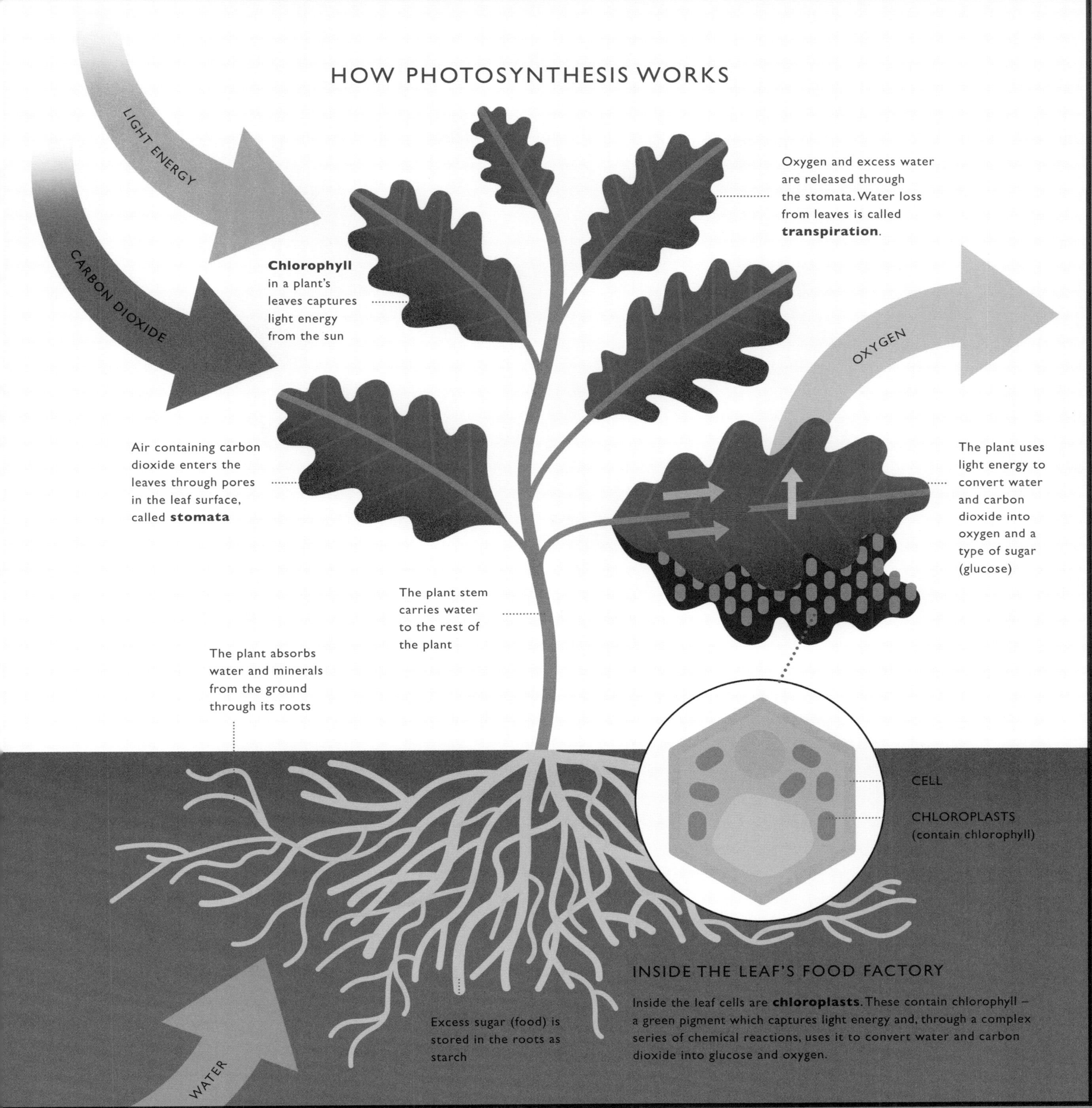

LIGHT ENERGY

CARBON DIOXIDE

OXYGEN

WATER

Chlorophyll in a plant's leaves captures light energy from the sun

Air containing carbon dioxide enters the leaves through pores in the leaf surface, called **stomata**

Oxygen and excess water are released through the stomata. Water loss from leaves is called **transpiration**.

The plant uses light energy to convert water and carbon dioxide into oxygen and a type of sugar (glucose)

The plant stem carries water to the rest of the plant

The plant absorbs water and minerals from the ground through its roots

Excess sugar (food) is stored in the roots as starch

CELL

CHLOROPLASTS (contain chlorophyll)

INSIDE THE LEAF'S FOOD FACTORY

Inside the leaf cells are **chloroplasts**. These contain chlorophyll — a green pigment which captures light energy and, through a complex series of chemical reactions, uses it to convert water and carbon dioxide into glucose and oxygen.

ALL ABOUT TREES

SOME TREES CAN GROW BIGGER THAN ANY OTHER PLANT AND LIVE LONGER THAN ANY ANIMAL ON EARTH. They provide food and shelter for thousands of living things. Their roots extend deep underground and hold the soil in place. Their leaves release oxygen for us to breathe. Without trees, life on our planet would find it hard to survive.

Bud — Leaf

Blossom

Twig — Fruit

THERE ARE TWO MAIN TYPES OF TREE:
evergreen and **deciduous**. Deciduous trees shed their leaves before the cold or dry season and grow new foliage in the spring. Evergreen trees keep their leaves year-round.

Deciduous maple tree   Evergreen Scots pine   Pine cone

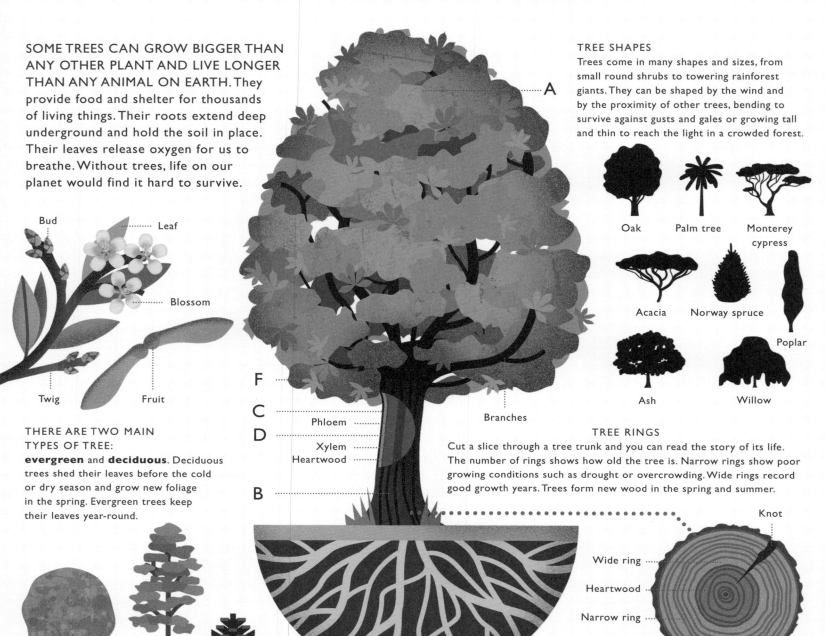

A

F
C
D

Phloem

Xylem
Heartwood

B

Branches

E

TREE SHAPES
Trees come in many shapes and sizes, from small round shrubs to towering rainforest giants. They can be shaped by the wind and by the proximity of other trees, bending to survive against gusts and gales or growing tall and thin to reach the light in a crowded forest.

Oak   Palm tree   Monterey cypress

Acacia   Norway spruce

Poplar

Ash   Willow

TREE RINGS
Cut a slice through a tree trunk and you can read the story of its life. The number of rings shows how old the tree is. Narrow rings show poor growing conditions such as drought or overcrowding. Wide rings record good growth years. Trees form new wood in the spring and summer.

Knot

Wide ring

Heartwood

Narrow ring

Sapwood

Bark

PARTS OF A TREE

A. **Crown** – The leaves and branches at the top of the tree. Each year, the tree increases in size by adding new twigs.

B. **Trunk/stem** – The trunk supports the crown and gives the tree its shape and strength. Sapwood (xylem) inside the trunk contains a network of tubes that runs between the roots and the leaves to provide water and nutrients from the soil.

C. **Bark** – The outer bark protects the tree from extreme temperatures, insect damage and disease; the inner bark (phloem) carries sugar and nutrients (sap) from the leaves to the rest of the tree. Bark can be smooth or rough. The bark of many trees changes colour and thickens as the tree ages.

D. **Cambium** – This forms new wood and produces growth rings.

E. **Roots** – The roots of a tree spread far and wide beyond its trunk through the surrounding soil. They absorb water and nutrients from the earth, store sugar, and anchor the tree in the ground.

F. **Leaves** – The leaves are every tree's main food factory. Through a process known as photosynthesis, they convert energy and chemicals taken from the sunlight, air and soil and convert it into food.

LEAF SHAPES

LEAF SHAPES ARE USEFUL WHEN IDENTIFYING TREES. In general, tropical plants tend to have simple shapes while those from temperate climates are more complex. Below you can see a selection of different types of leaf.

When using a leaf to identify a plant look not just at its colour, shape and texture, but also at the arrangement of the leaves on the stem, and at the way the edge of the leaf (known as the margin) is formed. Finally, consider the pattern made by the veins in the leaf. All of these factors can help to identify one plant's leaf from another.

PARTS OF A LEAF

Margin
Apex or tip
Midrib
Petiole
Base
Vein

Willow

Mountain ash

Oak

Horse chestnut

Sugar maple

Beech

Holly

Rhododendron

Scots pine

Cypress

Ginko

Philodendron (cheeseplant)

Bismark palm

Jade plant

FOOD CHAINS AND WEBS

IN THE HOT SUN OF THE AFRICAN SAVANNAH AN IMPALA GRAZES ON RED OAT GRASS. Minutes later, a lion attacks and the impala in turn becomes food for the big cat and the rest of his pride. This is an example of a simple **food chain** – a group of organisms linked in order of the food they eat.

Graphically, the food chain would look like this:

Red oat grass   Impala   Lion

Many food chains start with plants, living organisms that can make their own energy from the sun. They are the great **producers** of our world. The rest of the chain is made up of animal **consumers** that get their energy by consuming plants or other animals. There can sometimes be many of them in just one food chain.

A more complex food chain might look like this:

Red oat grass   Grasshopper   Baboon   Lion

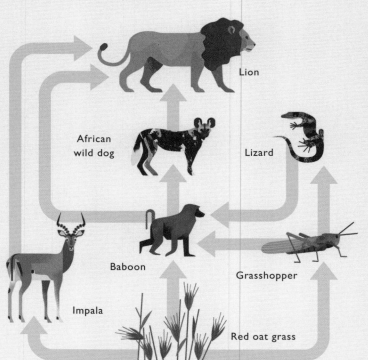

Lion

African wild dog   Lizard

Baboon   Grasshopper

Impala

Red oat grass

In most ecosystems the animals that live there rarely eat just one kind of food. This results in many different interlinked food chains known as **food webs**. You can see an example of a simple food web on the left.

• The arrows in a food chain or web represent the flow of energy between feeding – known as **trophic** – levels. At the end of the chain two other important groups of living things are at work…

• The first is the **scavengers** – creatures such as hyenas or vultures that eat dead or decaying meat.

• The second is the **decomposers**, such as bacteria or fungi, that break down any remaining animal or plant matter, thereby releasing its energy back into the soil so the chain can start all over again.

• If one part of the web is disturbed, for example if a species becomes extinct, the rest of the web will change as a result – sometimes with far-reaching consequences. Species in the food chain below the one that has become extinct may become more numerous, while those above it may struggle to find food and even die out themselves.

WHO EATS WHO IN THE AFRICAN SAVANNAH?

Apex predators – Usually large predatory carnivores, such as lions or leopards, which are not preyed upon by other creatures.

Scavengers – animals that eat dead or rotting flesh – for example, vultures and hyenas.

Secondary consumers – Predatory creatures that eat other animals (carnivores), or a mixture of animals and plants (omnivores) – for example, shrikes and baboons.

Primary consumers – herbivores that eat mainly plants – for example, grasshoppers or impalas.

Producers – organisms in the food chain that can produce their own energy and nutrients - for example, grasses or acacia trees.

Decomposers – organisms that break down dead plant and animal material and waste and release it as energy and nutrients back into the ecosystem – for example, bacteria or fungi.

Lions

APEX PREDATOR

SCAVENGER

Vulture

Shrike

Monitor lizard

SECONDARY CONSUMERS

Aardvark

African wild dog

TROPHIC LEVEL

Impala

Grasshopper

Wildebeest

PRIMARY CONSUMERS

Giraffe

Red oat grass

PRODUCERS

Fungi

Termite

DECOMPOSERS

Bacteria

Acacia

EXTRAORDINARY HUNTERS

IN THE SEARCH FOR THEIR NEXT MEAL, MANY ANIMALS – AND SOME PLANTS – HAVE EVOLVED SOPHISTICATED STRATEGIES TO CATCH THEIR PREY. Instead of relying on speed or stealth, some play the sit-and-wait game, often with some interesting enticements to lure their prey within easy reach. Others hunt communally, or build traps.

African wild dogs are the specialised pack hunters of the savannah. They employ different hunting techniques depending on the size and nature of their prey. Herding animals, such as antelope or wildebeest, will be rushed by the pack in order to isolate an individual. Some dogs will then run close to the target while others follow behind, ready to take over when the leaders tire. They will repeatedly bite larger prey during the chase until the animal eventually collapses from exhaustion and blood loss.

The **Anglerfish** lures its prey using a modified ray that protrudes from the front of its head and ends in a fleshy organ known as the esca. The fish uses this like a fishing rod, wiggling the lure to resemble a prey animal and grabbing anything that comes within reach of its huge mouth. Deep-sea species emit light from the lure thanks to the presence of bioluminescent bacteria that cause the lure to glow in the dark.

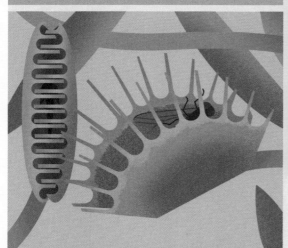

Humpback whales will often hunt communally, herding schools of fish towards the surface and then blowing a curtain of underwater bubbles around them. Once this effective bubble net is in place, the whales lunge upwards, open mouthed, to catch as many fish as possible before they scatter.

The **Venus flytrap** is a carnivorous plant that traps insects within its modified leaves. The trap is triggered when an insect comes into contact with special hairs on the inner surface of the leaf lobes that cause the trap to spring shut. The edges of the lobes then seal together to form a primitive kind of stomach, secreting enzymes so that the plant can digest the insect over the course of several days and absorb its nutrients.

The aptly named **archer fish** knocks insects off low-hanging vegetation above the water by shooting them down with a stream of spit. These fish rarely miss their target and can bring down prey up to 3 metres above the water's surface – impressive for a fish that is usually only 10 centimetres long.

The **ant lion** (the larva of a particular species of lacewing) digs its own sand-pit trap, burrowing down into the bottom with only its wide-open jaws projecting above the surface. Small insects such as ants that inadvertently stray over the edge of the pit can find no purchase on the steep slope of loose sand and slide straight down into the antlion's jaws.

Perhaps the most familiar webs are those spun by the **orb web spiders**. Once prey becomes entangled, they will inject it with paralysing venom and wrap it up in a silk cocoon before taking it to the edge of the web to be eaten. If their web gets damaged, they will eat the silk before spinning a new one.

Focus on Nature:

SPIDERS AND THEIR WEBS

HUNG WITH DEWDROPS ON AN AUTUMN MORNING A SPIDER WEB IS A THING OF BEAUTY, but it serves an important and usually deadly purpose – to trap a spider's insect prey.

• Spider silk is made in special silk glands attached to tiny organs on the spider's abdomen called **spinnerets**, although some kinds of tarantula also have silk glands in their feet.

• The silk is made from protein and is very elastic. It is even stronger than steel wire of the same thickness. Spiders can make several different kinds of silk depending on its purpose.

• Each strand of the web may be made of several strands of silk and some may be coated in a glue-like substance from the spider's abdomen to make them sticky.

• Different spiders make differently patterned webs. Some make messy webs called cobwebs while others spin nets that they drop on their prey.

Funnel-web spiders make funnel-shaped tunnels of silk in which they wait to ambush their prey. Some, like the Sydney funnel-web, have painful bites that can be fatal to humans.

Spiders also use silk to move about, raising or lowering themselves on silken strands.

Young spiders, called **spiderlings**, hatch from eggs protected by a silk cocoon.

The **water spider** uses its silk to build an underwater 'diving bell' that it fills with air and uses as a place to store prey and raise its young.

INTERESTING INSECTS

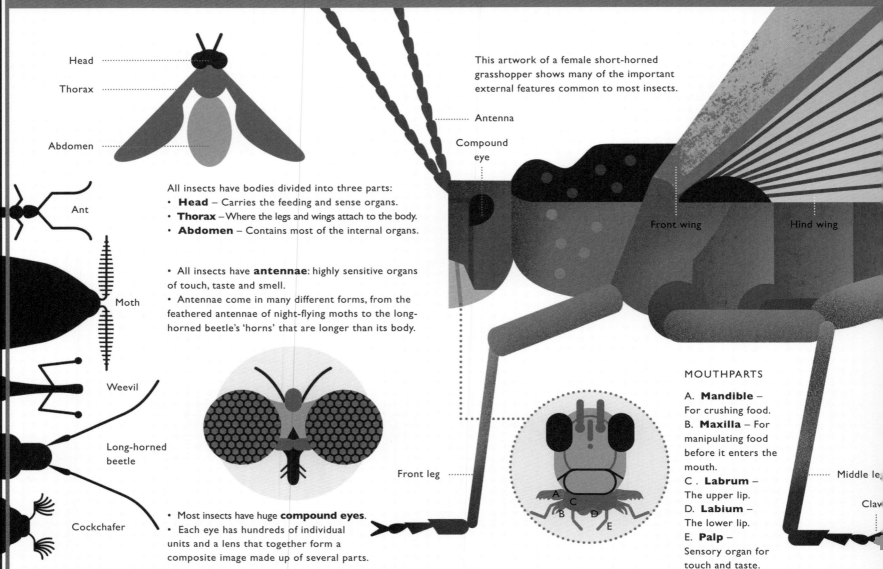

Head
Thorax
Abdomen

Ant

Moth

Weevil

Long-horned beetle

Cockchafer

All insects have bodies divided into three parts:
• **Head** – Carries the feeding and sense organs.
• **Thorax** – Where the legs and wings attach to the body.
• **Abdomen** – Contains most of the internal organs.

• All insects have **antennae**: highly sensitive organs of touch, taste and smell.
• Antennae come in many different forms, from the feathered antennae of night-flying moths to the long-horned beetle's 'horns' that are longer than its body.

• Most insects have huge **compound eyes**.
• Each eye has hundreds of individual units and a lens that together form a composite image made up of several parts.

This artwork of a female short-horned grasshopper shows many of the important external features common to most insects.

Antenna

Compound eye

Front wing

Hind wing

Front leg

Middle le[g]

Clav[...]

MOUTHPARTS

A. **Mandible** – For crushing food.
B. **Maxilla** – For manipulating food before it enters the mouth.
C. **Labrum** – The upper lip.
D. **Labium** – The lower lip.
E. **Palp** – Sensory organ for touch and taste.

MORE THAN HALF OF ALL KNOWN ANIMAL SPECIES ARE INSECTS. They are one of the most successful groups ever to have lived on our planet, with approximately a million different kinds already identified. No other animals can match them for their abundance and diversity.

• Insects are a class of arthropod invertebrates. They can be identified by their three pairs of legs and a body that is divided into three segments – the head, thorax and abdomen.

• All insects breathe air through openings called **spiracles** along the sides of their bodies. Even though some species, such as water beetles, live underwater, they still come to the surface to breathe.

• Many insects have wings – they are the only arthropods capable of flight – and this capability has allowed them to colonise a vast number of habitats.

• Insects lay eggs, sometimes in enormous numbers. Just one housefly could be responsible for millions of flies in a matter of

weeks, and this ability to breed very rapidly is one reason for the success of many insect species.

• Insects go through different stages between hatching and adulthood. Some undergo a dramatic change called **metamorphosis**. Others grow in steps, moulting their old exoskeleton, as they mature.

• Both adult insects and their larvae are food for many predators, from lizards and birds to mammals and even other insects. As a result they have developed a diverse range of strategies for defence and escape. Some attack their enemies with the help of poisonous bites or stings while others are designed to stay hidden. Predatory insects use many of the same techniques to catch their prey.

• Although some are considered to be pests, destroying crops, and spreading disease, insects play a vital role in life here on Earth. Without them, many other life forms would not exist. The majority of flowering plants depend on them for pollination and they are a major food source for many creatures.

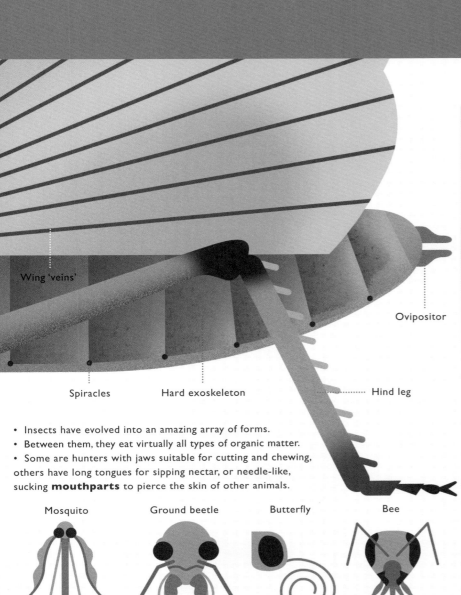

Wing 'veins'

Ovipositor

Spiracles   Hard exoskeleton   Hind leg

- Insects have evolved into an amazing array of forms.
- Between them, they eat virtually all types of organic matter.
- Some are hunters with jaws suitable for cutting and chewing, others have long tongues for sipping nectar, or needle-like, sucking **mouthparts** to pierce the skin of other animals.

Mosquito   Ground beetle   Butterfly   Bee

ARACHNIDS

Spiders and scorpions are not insects. They belong to a group of carnivorous, land-living arthropod invertebrates called **arachnids**. Unlike insects, arachnids have bodies divided into only two parts (the head and abdomen), and have eight legs and no antennae.

SCORPION

Stinger

Pincers   Head

Abdomen

Claws

SPIDER

Head

Spinnerets

Abdomen

Claws

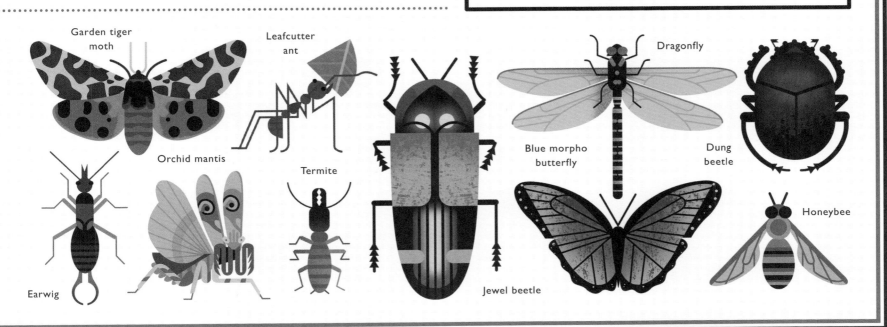

Garden tiger moth

Leafcutter ant

Dragonfly

Blue morpho butterfly

Dung beetle

Orchid mantis

Termite

Earwig

Jewel beetle

Honeybee

FLOWERING PLANTS

Next time you see a bee, look for a little bag of pollen attached to its back legs. Some species of bee use this structure, know as a pollen basket or corbicula, to help carry pollen back to their hive.

TAKE A GOOD LOOK AT A FLOWER – a buttercup is a good example. Inside the petals you'll find the stamens and the pistils by which the plant produces new seeds.

• Insects and other creatures are attracted to the flower because of its bright colour, its scent and by the nectar stored at the base of its petals. When they visit the flower, grains of pollen from the stamens get stuck their hairs, and they unintentionally carry the pollen to the carpel of the next flower they visit. This is called **pollination**. Watch a bee buzzing around inside a flower and you will see the pollen grains sticking to its hairy legs – pollination at work right before your eyes!

• Once a flower is pollinated, the new seeds will start to form in the ovary. This is called **fertilisation**.

• Some flowering plants are pollinated by the wind which blows their pollen from one plant to another.
• Other plants don't rely on pollination at all to make new plants. Instead, they send out long, thin stems, called runners, along the ground from which new plants develop. Plants like the strawberry do both.

PARTS OF A FLOWER

A. **Stamen** – Male part of the plant. It is formed from the **anther**. (B) which carries the pollen grains, and the **filament** (C).

D. **Pistil** – Female part of the plant. It is made up of many individual **carpels**.

E. **Carpel** – The sticky top part, which pollen

attaches to, is called a **stigma**.

F. **Ovary** – Contains **ovules**. Once fertilised by the pollen, these grow to form seeds.

G. **Petals** – Often coloured to attract visitors such as insects.

H. **Sepal** – Protects the flower bud.

ALL SORTS OF SEEDS

ONCE A FLOWER HAS BEEN FERTILISED, the petals die to leave behind a fruit with seeds. Some fruits are soft and full of juice, others are dry and hard. To give them their best chance of growing into new plants, the seeds need to be carried away from their parent plant to prevent overcrowding. This is called **dispersal**. There are four main ways in which plant seeds are dispersed – being blown away by the wind, carried by water, hitchhiking a ride on – or being eaten by – animals, and bursting or being thrown out of their

The fruits are light and feathery and get blown away by the wind, or shaken out of their seed pods by the motion of the plant.

Milkweed   Sycamore   Dandelion   Poppy

WIND

The fruits are juicy and are eaten by animals and dispersed in their droppings, or are covered in hairs or hooks and so get carried away on their fur.

Blackberry   Burdock   Acorn   Goosegrass

ANIMALS

The fruit pod dries up before splitting open and shooting the seeds out into the air to be carried away on the breeze.

Pea   Meadow cranesbill   Violet

BURSTING

The fruits float away before dropping down to the waterbed to take root. The coco de mer is the world's largest seed – so heavy that it cannot float so grows where it falls.

Mangrove   Lotus flower   Iris   Coco de mer

WATER

LIFE IN THE HONEYBEE HIVE

THE POPULATION OF A BEEHIVE IS MADE UP MOSTLY OF FEMALE WORKER BEES. They do not breed but instead are the tireless collectors of nectar and pollen, the queen's servants, nursemaids to the developing larvae and, lastly, the constructors and guardians of the hive itself.

• Each hive may contain up to 80,000 bees, and is ruled by the largest bee, the queen.

• The queen lays all of the eggs – as many as 2,000 a day if food is plentiful. She spends her whole life in the hive, attended by the worker bees that feed and clean her.

• Apart from the queen and the workers, the hive is also home to a few hundred short-lived male drone bees. Their entire purpose is to mate with the queen. Once their job is done, the drones will eventually be driven away from the hive by the worker bees to die.

• The hive is constructed from wax secreted by the worker bees and formed into combs made up of many six-sided cells. Some cells become **brood cells** – chambers for eggs and larvae. Others are used to store nectar, honey and pollen – the bees' main food during the summer. In the winter they feed from their honey store.

• Worker bees also look after the larvae, feeding them honey, nectar and royal jelly, a special substance made in glands on their heads. (Workers and drones only get a little, but developing queen larvae get lots!)

• When a hive gets overcrowded, the old queen will fly off to start a new colony, along with a few thousand workers. This behaviour is called swarming. Before she leaves, the old queen will lay some eggs in special, larger cells known as queen cups. The first queen to hatch from these will kill her unborn rivals before taking control of the hive.

• Not all bees live in communal hives. Some species are solitary, and others are parasitic, laying their eggs inside the larvae of other insects.

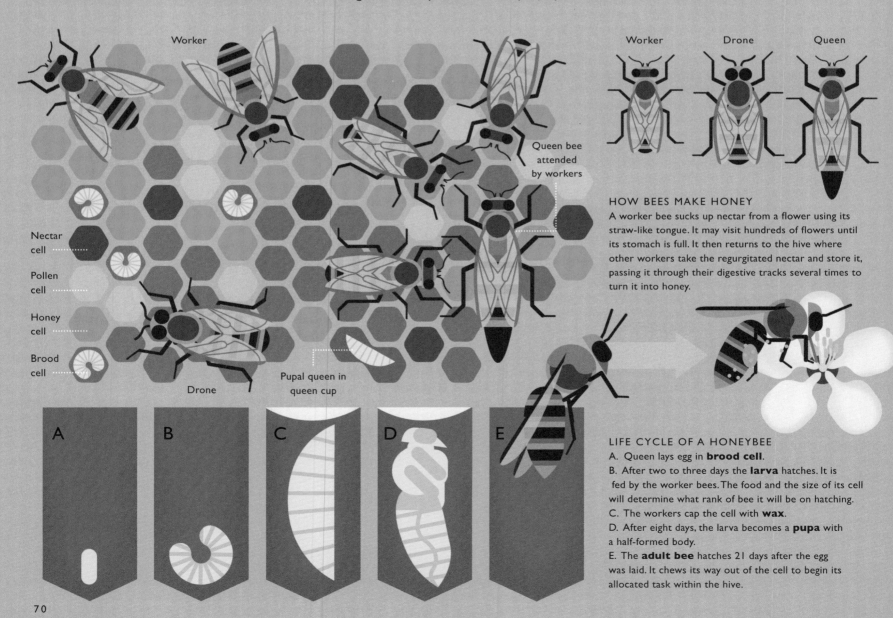

HOW BEES MAKE HONEY

A worker bee sucks up nectar from a flower using its straw-like tongue. It may visit hundreds of flowers until its stomach is full. It then returns to the hive where other workers take the regurgitated nectar and store it, passing it through their digestive tracks several times to turn it into honey.

LIFE CYCLE OF A HONEYBEE

A. Queen lays egg in **brood cell**.

B. After two to three days the **larva** hatches. It is fed by the worker bees. The food and the size of its cell will determine what rank of bee it will be on hatching.

C. The workers cap the cell with **wax**.

D. After eight days, the larva becomes a **pupa** with a half-formed body.

E. The **adult bee** hatches 21 days after the egg was laid. It chews its way out of the cell to begin its allocated task within the hive.

ANIMAL ARCHITECTS

THE NATURAL WORLD IS FULL OF STRUCTURES BUILT BY ANIMALS. From the simple to the highly elaborate, they are created primarily for one of three reasons: as a home that provides protection; as a trap to catch prey or store food; or to communicate with others of their kind – particularly to attract a mate as in the case of the remarkable bower bird.

• Some animal homes are amazingly complex structures that provide not only protection from predators, but a place in which the animals can breed and raise their young, store food and find shelter – from the harsh cold of winter to the burning sun of the tropics.

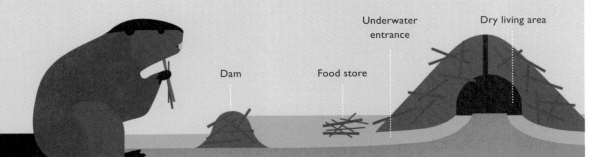

Beavers are skilful engineers, constructing dams across rivers and streams in order to create deep pools in which they build their homes, called lodges. Built from branches, sticks and mud, these lodges are so strong that even bears cannot break into them.

Dam

Food store

Underwater entrance

Dry living area

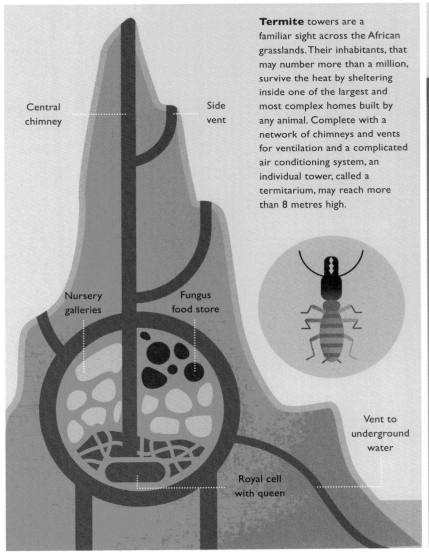

Termite towers are a familiar sight across the African grasslands. Their inhabitants, that may number more than a million, survive the heat by sheltering inside one of the largest and most complex homes built by any animal. Complete with a network of chimneys and vents for ventilation and a complicated air conditioning system, an individual tower, called a termitarium, may reach more than 8 metres high.

Central chimney

Side vent

Nursery galleries

Fungus food store

Vent to underground water

Royal cell with queen

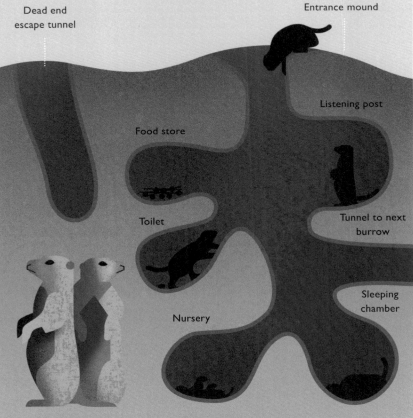

Dead end escape tunnel

Entrance mound

Listening post

Food store

Toilet

Tunnel to next burrow

Sleeping chamber

Nursery

Prairie dogs dig extensive warrens, sometimes covering thousands of square metres. These so-called 'towns' are made up of many individual burrows, each with separate chambers designated for sleeping, raising young and even toilets, plus special listening posts that are dug near exits so the owners can listen for predators before emerging. In winter, these rodents hibernate in their burrows for many months coming out to feed only on warmer days.

Journey through Nature:

A RIVER JOURNEY

CANADA IS A LAND TRANSFORMED BY WATER, from the white-water cascades that thunder through its glacier-carved valleys, to the maze of rivers, lakes, ponds and bogs that criss-cross its ancient evergreen forests. Formed over millions of years, its wetland habitats and long meandering rivers run through boreal forest, windswept prairies and huge mud-filled deltas, providing food and shelter for animals of all kinds. Hundreds of species live among this watery wilderness, from the majestic grizzly bear to the industrious beaver, depending on the rivers and their surrounding wetlands for food and shelter. You can find out more about the wetland creatures shown here over the page.

WHO LIVES HERE?

RIVERS ARE A KEY PART OF THE WATER CYCLE OF OUR PLANET. They help carry water and nutrients all around the Earth and drain over 75% of the land's surface. Many types of creature live in and around rivers, building homes within the banks, living on the islands that occur within the waters, or colonising one of the many different wetland habitats that occur along any river's path to the ocean.

Most rivers have an **upper**, **middle** and **lower** course.
• At their **source**, usually on high ground, the river has a rapid, tumbling flow, cutting a narrow channel through the land.
• Along its **middle**, the river gets wider, slower, and follows a meandering path.
• Over time, **lakes** may appear and areas of **marsh** form where the river floods.
• Where the current slows it drops its heavy sediment to form **sand** bars or small islands.
• As it reaches the sea the river may be very wide and slow moving.
• At its mouth, a **delta** may form, where shallow channels are separated by a maze of mudbanks.

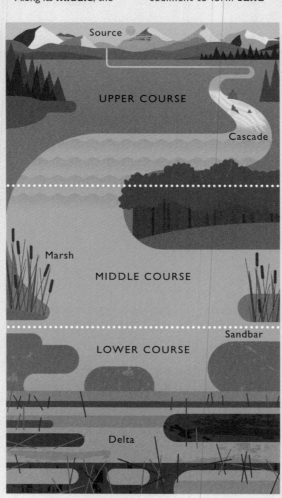

A. **Bald eagle** – An expert fisher, this majestic bird of prey swoops low over the water surface, catching fish in its talons.

B. **Chinook salmon** – Also known as king salmon, chinooks swimming up Canada's Yukon River travel more than 3,000 kilometres from the Bering Sea.

C. **Fisher** – This weasel relative eats small mammals, birds and even porcupines!

D. **Grizzly bear** – Large numbers gather by the river in spring to feed on spawning salmon, fighting for the best fishing spots.

E. **River otter** – Well-adapted for swimming, the otter has webbed feet and nostrils and ears that close when underwater.

F. **Beaver** – These greatly alter the river environment by building lodges and dams. Many generations of beaver may use a single dam until it finally fills up with silt forcing them to move home.

G. **Painted turtle** – Found in lakes, ponds and slow-moving rivers, this freshwater turtle is widespread in North America.

H. **Blue jay** – This bird feeds mainly on nuts and seeds but hunts for insects and other invertebrates at the river's edge.

I. **Flathead catfish** – Inhabiting deep pools, lakes and slow-moving rivers, these voracious predators can grow to over 1.5 metres in length.

J. **Lake sturgeon** – This large species of fish stirs up the the riverbed with its spade-like snout and then uses the sensory barbels dangling near its mouth to locate its prey.

K. **Loon** – Its webbed feet allow the loon to propel itself through the water catching its prey with its long stabbing beak.

L. **Canvasback** – are the largest diving duck in North America.

M. **Moose** – These feed on large quantities of aquatic vegetation for sodium content.

N. **American bullfrog** – These giants may reach up to 20 centimetres in length.

O. **Muskrat** – Great wetland builders, they construct feeding platforms and nests to protect their young from cold and predators.

P. **Belted kingfisher** – Spot them perched on a branch watch point looking out for fish.

Q. **Whooping crane** – They probe the mud with their bills in search of small crustaceans and molluscs.

R. **Snow goose** – Great flocks of these geese over-winter on coastal marshes.

S. **Northern pintails** – These are named for their long central tail feathers.

T. **Trumpeter swan** – These huge birds are named after their loud, musical calls.

U. **Canada goose** – Spot each bird taking a turn to fly at the front of their distinctive V-shaped formation, as they share this energy consuming task.

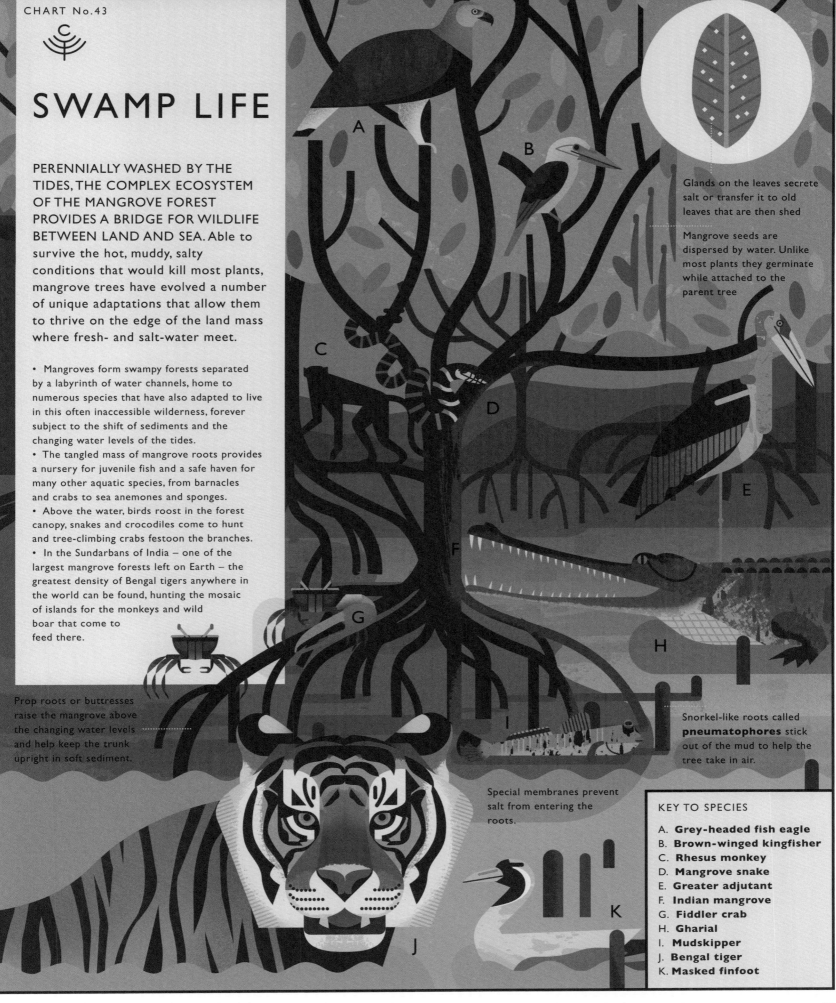

SWAMP LIFE

PERENNIALLY WASHED BY THE TIDES, THE COMPLEX ECOSYSTEM OF THE MANGROVE FOREST PROVIDES A BRIDGE FOR WILDLIFE BETWEEN LAND AND SEA. Able to survive the hot, muddy, salty conditions that would kill most plants, mangrove trees have evolved a number of unique adaptations that allow them to thrive on the edge of the land mass where fresh- and salt-water meet.

• Mangroves form swampy forests separated by a labyrinth of water channels, home to numerous species that have also adapted to live in this often inaccessible wilderness, forever subject to the shift of sediments and the changing water levels of the tides.
• The tangled mass of mangrove roots provides a nursery for juvenile fish and a safe haven for many other aquatic species, from barnacles and crabs to sea anemones and sponges.
• Above the water, birds roost in the forest canopy, snakes and crocodiles come to hunt and tree-climbing crabs festoon the branches.
• In the Sundarbans of India – one of the largest mangrove forests left on Earth – the greatest density of Bengal tigers anywhere in the world can be found, hunting the mosaic of islands for the monkeys and wild boar that come to feed there.

Glands on the leaves secrete salt or transfer it to old leaves that are then shed

Mangrove seeds are dispersed by water. Unlike most plants they germinate while attached to the parent tree

Prop roots or buttresses raise the mangrove above the changing water levels and help keep the trunk upright in soft sediment.

Snorkel-like roots called **pneumatophores** stick out of the mud to help the tree take in air.

Special membranes prevent salt from entering the roots.

KEY TO SPECIES

A. **Grey-headed fish eagle**
B. **Brown-winged kingfisher**
C. **Rhesus monkey**
D. **Mangrove snake**
E. **Greater adjutant**
F. **Indian mangrove**
G. **Fiddler crab**
H. **Gharial**
I. **Mudskipper**
J. **Bengal tiger**
K. **Masked finfoot**

ALL ABOUT AMPHIBIANS

FROM BRIGHTLY COLOURED FROGS AND TOADS TO SLIPPERY SALAMANDERS, AMPHIBIANS ARE SOME OF EARTH'S MOST COLOURFUL CREATURES. These cold-blooded vertebrates are divided into three groups – newts and salamanders, frogs and toads and the less familiar, worm-like caecilians. Many live close to fresh water in tropical or temperate regions although some have adapted to live a more land-based lifestyle.

• Modern amphibians first appeared more than 300 million years ago, the descendants of early fleshy-finned fish.
• They are well adapted to live both in and out of water. Many species begin life as aquatic larvae that breathe using gills and then transform through metamorphosis into terrestrial adults that take in oxygen using lungs. Others, especially tropical species, do not have an aquatic larval stage and some do not lay eggs but give birth to live young.

• The skin of amphibians is a vitally important organ. It is permeable, allowing water to pass through, and is kept moist by numerous mucus glands; it is also used to take in oxygen. Some species have no lungs at all and breathe entirely through their skin and the lining of their mouths.
• Many amphibians also produce secretions through their skin that taste horrid or are poisonous. Highly toxic species often advertise this fact by being brightly coloured.

Newts and salamanders most closely resemble the creatures from which all living amphibians are descended and have very varied life cycles. Newts spend much of their life on land, returning to the water to breed while some salamanders spend all of their lives in water, other wholly on land. Most are small but the Chinese giant salamander, the largest amphibian in the world, can reach lengths of nearly 2 metres.

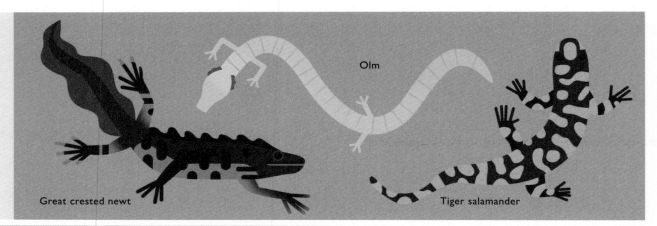

Great crested newt

Olm

Tiger salamander

Red-eyed tree frog

Common frog

Common toad

Javan gliding frog

Fire-bellied toad

Frogs and toads are probably the best known of all amphibians and form by far the largest group, with 6,500 known living species. Most live in damp habitats and return to fresh water to lay their spawn. Some species have adapted to burrow in the earth, and have evolved horny growths on their back feet to help in their excavations. Others species have sticky pads on the ends of their fingers and toes to help them climb trees, while those that spend much time in the water have webbing to help them swim more effectively. Famous for their ability to jump out of the way of danger, many also have brightly coloured markings to advertise their nasty taste or rely on camouflage to protect them against predation.

Elusive and mostly tropical **caecilians** usually stay hidden underground or underwater. With no limbs and skin divided into rings around their long bodies, they are often mistaken for a worm. Most live in tropical forests, buried in moist leaf litter and soil where they hunt using their sense of smell.

FROG FEET

ADAPTED FOR
SWIMMING
Webbing

ADAPTED FOR CLIMBING
Adhesive pads
Widely spread toes

ADAPTED FOR
DIGGING
Horny growth

WHAT'S IN THE POND?

LOOK BELOW THE STILL SURFACE WATER OF A POND IN SPRING AND YOU WILL FIND A WORLD TEEMING WITH WILDLIFE. In temperate climates the arrival of warmer weather and longer days heralds a burst of colour and activity, as many different creatures get busy after the long, slow months of winter. Spring flowers come into bloom, attracting pollinators with their showy petals. Many creatures are transformed by bright breeding colours, from the glossy green head of the male mallard to the fiery red belly of the three-spined stickleback. Under a microscope, the pond water reveals a further abundance of tiny life, including the larvae of many aquatic insects – an important source of food for many creatures.

48

KEY TO SPECIES

A. **Damselfly**
B. **Dragonfly nymph**
C. **Reedmace**
D. **Natterjack toad**
E. **Yellow water lily**

F. **Mallard** (female)
G. **Mallard** (male)
H. **Hawker dragonfly**
I. **Water boatman**
J. **Yellow flag**

K. **Marsh marigold**
L. **Water flea**
M. **Great crested newt** (male)
N. **Great crested newt** (female)
O. **Pondweed**

P. **Mosquito larva**
Q. **Ramshorn snail**
R. **Three-spined stickleback** (male)
S. **Great diving beetle**

WILD ROMANCE

FINDING THE RIGHT PARTNER IS AN IMPORTANT PART OF THE SURVIVAL STRATEGY OF MANY SPECIES. Breeding with the strongest, smartest mate is the best way for any creature to ensure their offspring have the greatest chance of surviving to find mates of their own.
• For animals that live in groups finding a partner is seldom a problem. Here, the mating game mainly involves competition between rival males, sometimes fighting to the death, to win the right to mate, often with several females. The rutting of red deer, the bloody body blows traded by bull elephant seals and the head-to-head clashes between rival warthogs are all nature's way of ensuring that it is only the fittest males who sire the next generation of young.

FOR ANIMALS THAT ARE MAINLY SOLITARY, A MATE MUST FIRST BE LOCATED and then one of the sexes, usually the male, needs to demonstrate his suitability as a partner before mating can take place. This process is known as **courtship**.
• Some species locate potential mates by sending out simple sensory signals, such as the pheromones produced by female moths that can be smelt by males over several miles, or the courtship song of many types of frog.
• Other species rely on visual signals to help them win over a partner, with many developing bright colours during the breeding season to attract the opposite sex. In almost all cases it is the male who does this while the female remains drably coloured – a useful camouflage which will help to protect her while raising young.

The male **great crested newt** develops a large jagged crest along his back during the breeding season to help him attract a female. During spring, he will flash his bright orange belly in a courtship display as he patrols his underwater territory.

The male **frigate bird** has an eye-catching throat pouch that he inflates to great effect to draw the attention of watching females. Unlike some other animals, birds have good colour vision which is why so many males have evolved colourful plumage as part of their courtship strategy.

Great crested grebes are well known for their courtship *pas de deux* in which both partners will raise their head crests and puff out their ruffs before beginning their elaborate dance. After much head shaking, touching of beaks and mutual bowing, the birds will dive at the same time for vegetation and then rise high out of the water, furiously paddling their feet to remain aloft while they offer each other their gifts of weed. After successful mating, both adults will help make the nest and rear the chicks, teaching them to dive for food and carrying them on their backs until they are old enough to fend for themselves.

In an accomplished display of courtship and construction, the male **Vogelkop bowerbird** builds an elaborate bower of sticks, before decorating the entrance with colour co-ordinated piles of collected objects. Berries, flowers, beetle wings, even bottle tops if they are the right colour, will be meticulously arranged over several days. The bower is purely built for the purpose of courtship. If the male wins the attention of a female and mating occurs, she will build a simpler nest elsewhere in which to lay her eggs.

The male **peacock spider** raises the colourful flap on his abdomen in the hope of attracting the attention of his much larger female mate. He will vibrate his abdomen to gain her attention, waving his legs over his head and dancing from side to side. For him, much more than successful mating is at stake – if he is not sufficiently impressive with his dance moves, his prospective partner may well eat him!

HEAVENLY DANCERS

NOWHERE IS COURTSHIP TAKEN TO MORE SPECTACULAR VISUAL EXTREMES THAN IN THE MATING DANCE OF THE BIRDS OF PARADISE. With their ornate plumage, percussive calls and extraordinary body movements, the males seek to catch the eye of a mate with some of the most elaborate courtship displays on Earth.

• There are 41 different species, the majority of which live in the rainforests of New Guinea and its surrounding islands.

• The mating antics of the males include flicking and quivering their feathers to form giant ruffs or fans, jumping, dancing and hanging upside down, with their dance moves often accompanied by loud calls.

• The courtship displays are enhanced by the male's vibrant plumage with feathers that often incorporate metallic or iridescent patches, or long head- or tail-plumes.

• Unlike the males, female birds of paradise are usually plain in colour and lack the feathery ornamentation of their partners. Once they have chosen their mate, they will build a simple nest and raise their young alone.

• Scientists have speculated that the scarcity of natural predators in their environment may be one reason why these birds have evolved such complex and flamboyant mating rituals – the result of thousands of years of undisturbed competition for female favour.

E

D

F

Male superb bird of paradise in full courtship display

F

KEY TO SPECIES

A. **Raggiana bird of paradise** – Male birds gather in trees in large groups of up to 20 individuals to display in front of watching females, calling loudly while quivering their long, lacy tail feathers over their heads.

B. **King of Saxony bird of paradise** – This bird has immensely long head-plumes which he will swing through an arc of 180 degrees as part of his display, sitting in the top of a tree specially selected for the purpose of his mating performance.

C. **Six-plumed bird of paradise** – Before beginning his solo courtship dance, the male of this species clears a display area on the ground. Looking a little like a ballerina in a tutu, he fluffs out his long neck feathers into a 'skirt' and flicks the iridescent ones on his throat up and down, before hopping from one foot to the other and waggling his head-plumes in a virtuoso performance.

D. **Male king bird of paradise** – In courtship, this bird puffs himself up into a feathery ball before waving his brilliantly-tipped tail feathers over his head. At 14 centimetres they are almost as long as his body.

E. **Magnificent riflebird** – This bird dances for his mate up and down a branch, flicking his head from side to side to expose his iridescent throat feathers, while vibrating his open wings in a noisy display.

F. **Superb bird of paradise** – In one of the most extraordinary of all courtship rituals, the male uses his chest and neck feathers to create an enormous mask, complete with neon markings, with which to impress his mate. As part of this curious spectacle he dances back and forth, making loud clicking noises in the hope that his mate will see him as a suitable suitor.

Female superb bird of paradise in nest

ALL KINDS OF NESTS

MANY DIFFERENT KINDS OF ANIMAL MAKE NESTS, collecting a variety of building materials and fashioning them carefully into a structure where they can shelter or bring up their young. Birds' nests are probably the best known and most varied, ranging from a stork's untidy pile of sticks to a songbird's intricately woven basket. Fish often make nests in a similar way, while mammals and insects often choose burrows over nests as a place to call home.

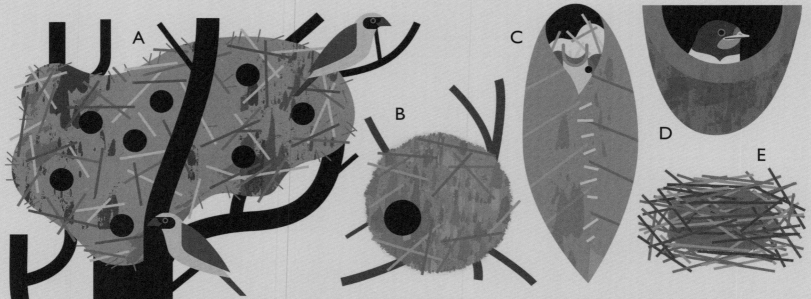

A. **Sociable weaver bird nest** – Some animals make communal nests and this African bird makes giant constructions of grass that can house several hundred pairs. Each breeding pair has its own separate compartment within the nest, and these high-rise apartments can sometimes get so heavy that they bring down the trees in which they are built.

B. **Long-tailed tit nest** – This cup nest is formed from lichen, feathers, spider silk and moss, often using many thousands of individual fibres to form the tiny structure. The bird will cover the outside of the nest with hundreds of lichen flakes to camouflage it before lining it with its own feathery down to provide a comfy place to lay its eggs.

C. **Common tailorbird nest** – This cradle is formed by sewing together large leaves with plant fibres or spider silk. The bird carefully fashions its nest so that the leaves face outwards, providing plenty of camouflage.

D. **Swallow nest** – One of several species of bird that builds mud nests, the swallow scoops up wet mud in its beak before fashioning it into cup-shaped nests attached under the eaves of buildings.

E. **White stork nest** – Many large birds make untidy nests of sticks. Stork nests are often made near human habitation, on the roofs of tall buildings. The birds return to the same nest year after year.

The male **three-spined stickleback** will dig a small pit in the riverbed before filling it with plant material to make his tunnel nest. Once complete, he will court a female with a zigzag dance until she swims through the tunnel to deposit her eggs in the nest where he will then fertilise them.

All **wasps** build nests, whether to house the eggs of a solitary wasp or as a home for a social colony. Unlike the waxy hives made by bees, wasps often make their papery shelters from wood fibres, scraped away by their hard mandibles and chewed into a pulp.

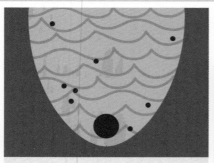

Spiders and some other insects use silk to form a cocoon, often attached to plants, in which they lay their eggs.

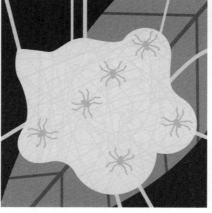

The **dormouse** spends much of its life asleep. In the winter it will hibernate in a nest on the ground in the base of a tree or under a log pile but in summer it will weave a nest of bark, leaves and grasses among the undergrowth. If food is scarce or the weather is cold and wet, it will save energy by curling up in a ball and sleeping until conditions improve.

ALL KINDS OF EGGS

OF ALL THE EGGS LAID BY ANIMALS, BIRDS' EGGS ARE PROBABLY THE BEST KNOWN. Their hard shells protect the growing embryo inside and although these can be white in colour from the calcium carbonate from which the shell is made, various pigments can cause the shell to take on different colours and patterns. Tree-nesting birds are more likely to have blue or green eggs, while birds that nest near or on the ground often have eggs with patterned shells to help with camouflage.

Skate egg case
9cm

Terrapin egg
4cm

Horn shark egg case
11cm

Common frogspawn
1cm

Butterfly eggs
1–3mm

- The largest living bird's egg is that of the ostrich, measuring 15 centimetres in length. The smallest is laid by the bee humming-bird and is no bigger than a pea.
- Guillemots' eggs, as well as those of other birds who nest on cliff ledges, are shaped with a pronounced point at one end so they roll in a tight circle, protected by their own dynamics from falling over the edge.
- Unlike birds' eggs that are incubated by the parent until they hatch, the leathery eggs of reptiles are often buried underground with the young often fending for themselves once hatched.
- The eggs of many fish and amphibians (known as spawn) are jelly-like and laid in water. Often large numbers of eggs will be laid at one time and, in the case of most species, will be fertilised by the male only after they have been laid.
- The fertilised eggs of some species of shark are laid within a protective egg case. Once the fish hatch, the egg cases can often be found washed up on the beach where they are commonly known as mermaid's purses.
- Many invertebrates lay eggs, including insects, spiders, molluscs and crustaceans. Insect eggs in particular come in many different shapes and colours and are often laid en masse on the underside of plant leaves.
- The eggs of egg-laying mammals, or monotremes, are laid in burrows and have leathery shells similar to the eggs of reptiles.

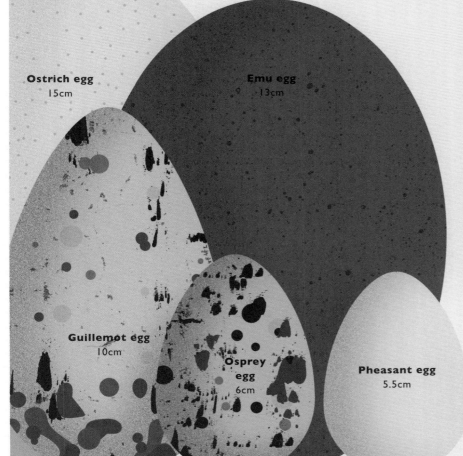

Ostrich egg
15cm

Emu egg
13cm

Guillemot egg
10cm

Osprey egg
6cm

Pheasant egg
5.5cm

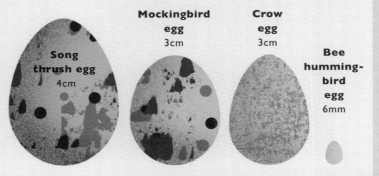

Song thrush egg
4cm

Mockingbird egg
3cm

Crow egg
3cm

Bee humming-bird egg
6mm

Focus on Nature:
THE PECULIAR PLATYPUS

THE DUCK-BILLED PLATYPUS, along with its close relatives the echidnas, make up a group of creatures known as **monotremes** – the only mammals to lay eggs. It is one of the most curious of all animals, with its beak-shaped snout, beaver-like tail and webbed feet, all attached to a compact body covered in plum-coloured dense, waterproof fur.

• The platypus lives in the rivers of Eastern Australia where it makes a bankside burrow in which to lay its one or two leathery-shelled eggs.

• Once hatched, the young are suckled for three to four months by their mother who will leave them sealed into the nest for over 24 hours while she goes foraging, probing the riverbed for small aquatic prey.

Males have poison spur on hind foot, used for fighting rivals

Webbed feet

Plush mole-like fur

Eyes and ears close when diving underwater

Highly sensitive beak covered in rubbery skin

Beak can detect water-borne electrical signals from the muscles of small aquatic animals

Leathery-shelled eggs

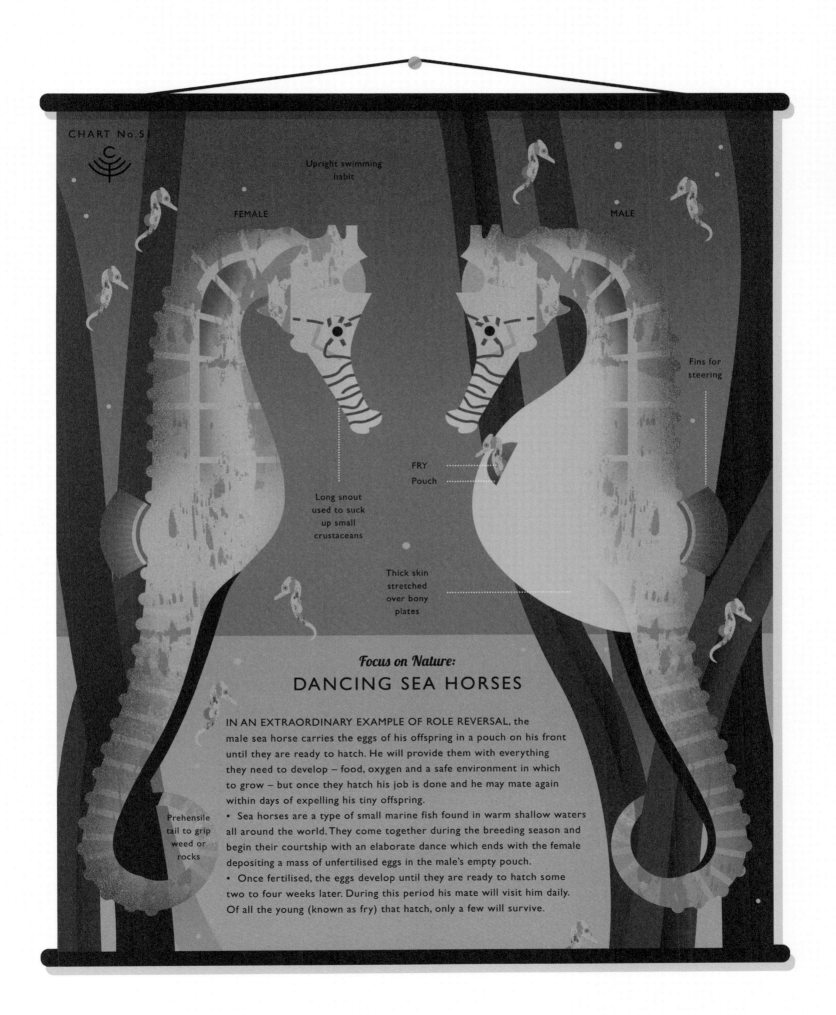

CHART No.51

Upright swimming habit

FEMALE

MALE

Fins for steering

FRY
Pouch

Long snout used to suck up small crustaceans

Thick skin stretched over bony plates

Prehensile tail to grip weed or rocks

Focus on Nature:
DANCING SEA HORSES

IN AN EXTRAORDINARY EXAMPLE OF ROLE REVERSAL, the male sea horse carries the eggs of his offspring in a pouch on his front until they are ready to hatch. He will provide them with everything they need to develop – food, oxygen and a safe environment in which to grow – but once they hatch his job is done and he may mate again within days of expelling his tiny offspring.

• Sea horses are a type of small marine fish found in warm shallow waters all around the world. They come together during the breeding season and begin their courtship with an elaborate dance which ends with the female depositing a mass of unfertilised eggs in the male's empty pouch.

• Once fertilised, the eggs develop until they are ready to hatch some two to four weeks later. During this period his mate will visit him daily. Of all the young (known as fry) that hatch, only a few will survive.

LIVING TO

FOR MANY ANIMALS, LIVING TOGETHER WITH OTHERS OF THEIR KIND IS AN IMPORTANT PART OF SURVIVAL. While some creatures live a largely solitary existence, perhaps only coming together to mate, many others form social groups. These groups can vary in size from those containing just a few individuals to many hundreds. They may last for only a few days, in the case of insect swarms, or be based on family bonds that are maintained for a lifetime.

Orcas are highly social whales that live in family groups, called pods, of up to 30 individuals revolving around a central female. Newborn calves may be looked after by the whole pod but will retain a lifelong bond with their mother, remaining with the pod and adding to its numbers with offspring of their own.

Grazing animals such as **zebra** often live together in groups of many individuals called herds. In habitats where there is little protection against hunters, living together in this way gives the animals a better chance of survival – predators find it difficult to single out individuals to attack and there are always many eyes alert for signs of danger. Living in large groups like this is common among many kinds of prey animal.

Even when animals choose to live together in families or larger groups, most continue to function as individual units. However, some kinds of invertebrates have evolved to become permanently linked together in the formation of complex colonies. The most important colonial animals are the reef-building **corals** – thousands of individual polyps that together form the coral reefs that provide a home for many other creatures.

GETHER

Wolves live in small family groups known as packs, usually consisting of eight to twelve individuals. The pack has a strong hierarchy that centres around the dominant male and female – the only members of the group that breed each year. The rest of the pack is made up of offspring from previous years who may remain with their parents for some time and help care for the new cubs. By hunting in packs, wolves can tackle creatures much bigger than themselves, which increases their range of prey as well as their likelihood of success. Each pack will define and defend its territory by scent marking the boundaries and howling to announce its presence to rivals.

Bees, like their close relatives ants and termites, live in highly organised colonies of up to 80,000 creatures, where just one member – the queen – produces all the young. The other members of the colony have clearly defined roles, all working together so that they behave more like a single organism than hundreds – or thousands – of individuals.

Although the **Portuguese man-of-war** looks like an individual animal, it is in fact a colony made up of several different creatures, called polyps. Each type of polyp has its own distinct role such as catching or digesting food, reproducing, or forming the gas-filled bubble that keeps the colony afloat.

Every other year the **wandering albatross** returns to its original nesting site after months spent in solitary flight over the world's oceans. There it will find its mate, picking them out from hundreds of other individuals thanks to its acute sense of smell. The birds pair for life and, after an elaborate courtship display to re-establish their bond, will raise their single chick together for over nine months before going their separate ways until the next breeding season.

FANTASTIC FISH

FISH WERE THE FIRST ANIMALS WITH A BACKBONE TO APPEAR ON THE PLANET, around 500 million years ago.
• Fish do not form a natural group in classification – instead, some fish are more closely related to other vertebrates than they are to other fish.
• There are over 30,000 species, varying hugely in size and shape, from tiny minnows of less than a centimetre to huge whale sharks of over 15 metres.
• Fish are found in many aquatic environments, from mountain streams to ocean trenches. Some, like salmon, migrate between salt- and freshwater.
• Living fish are divided into four major groups: **jawless fish** (hagfish and lampreys),

cartilaginous fish (sharks and rays), **ray-finned fish** (including 'typical' bony fish) and **lobe-finned fish**. Ray-finned fish are by far the biggest group.
• All fish are cold-blooded which allows their temperature to fluctuate with outside conditions.
• They breathe by extracting oxygen from the water using their gills.
• Most are streamlined in shape, have a tail fin to help propel them through the water, fins for steering, and scales for protection, although some, such as eels and lampreys, have a covering of tough skin.
• With the exception of some that give birth to live young, most fish lay eggs.

DIAGRAM OF A RAY-FINNED FISH

THE LIVING REEF

Nowhere on Earth will you find a greater number of fish species than in the underwater 'rainforest' of a coral reef. Built from the bodies of billions of tiny creatures called coral polyps, reefs provide a home to thousands of different creatures and are found in warm, shallow waters all round the world. The largest is the Great Barrier Reef, found off the southern coast of Australia. At 2,000 kilometres long it is the biggest structure made by living organisms – so large that it can even be seen from space.

KEY TO SPECIES

A. **Reef shark**
B. **Angelfish**
C. **Green turtle**
D. **Butterfly fish**
E. **Sea snake**
F. **Dugong**
G. **Surgeon fish**
H. **Clownfish**
I. **Moray eel**
J. **Parrotfish**
K. **Box jellyfish**
L. **Starfish**
M. **Crown of thorns starfish**
N. **Sea anemone**
O. **Nudibranch or sea slug**
P. **Blue-ringed octopus**
Q. **Lionfish**
R. **Conesnail**
S. **Sponge**
T. **Tube sponge**
U. **Sea horse**
V. **Triggerfish**
W. **Coral**

A PERFECT PARTNERSHIP

THE CLOWNFISH AND THE SEA ANEMONE are a good example of a mutual **symbiotic** relationship where both creatures, although completely different species, live side by side and benefit from each other's presence.

• The sea anemone's stinging tentacles protect the clownfish from predators and provide a safe nesting site for the fish's eggs and young. A special mucus coating its scales makes it immune to stings.

• The clownfish feeds on the anemone's leftovers.

• In return, the anemone is defended by the clownfish from predators and parasites, and uses nutrients from the clownfish's nitrogen-rich excrement to grow new tentacles and repair damaged tissue.

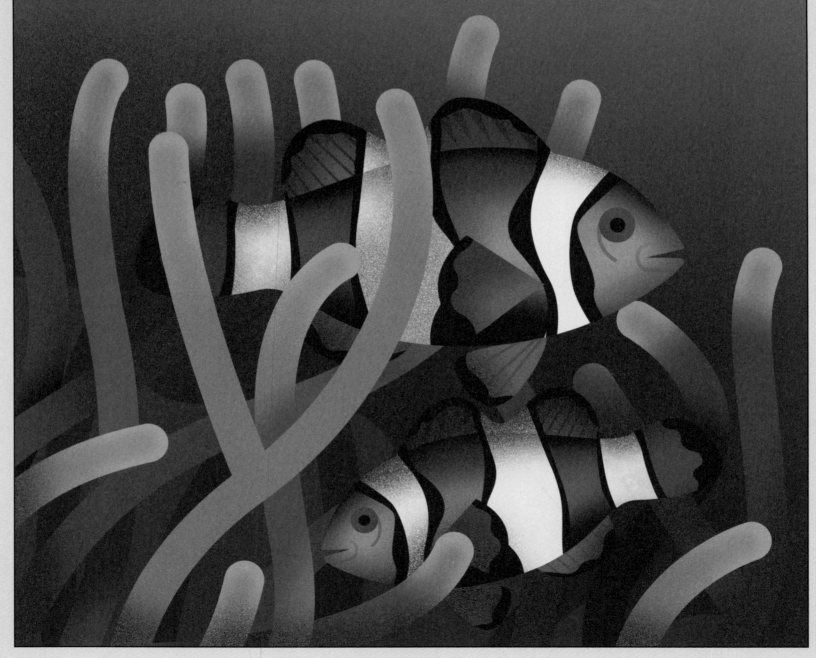

MARINE INVERTEBRATES

INVERTEBRATES MAKE UP 97% OF THE WORLD'S KNOWN ANIMAL SPECIES. A great many live in the sea, from tiny shrimps to giant squid, colourful corals to spiky sea urchins. Some have soft bodies and have developed an ingenious array of survival strategies to defend themselves from predators. Others, like the crabs, lobsters and shrimps, have a hard exoskeleton for protection, much like their land-dwelling cousins, the insects.

CNIDARIANS

Cnidarians include the sea anemones, jellyfish and corals. They have hollow, bell-shaped bodies and a central mouth ringed by highly sensitive tentacles. The tentacles are armed with stinging cells, called nemotocycsts that fire poison-tipped threads into anything that brushes against them.

CRUSTACEANS

The marine crustaceans include lobsters, crabs and shrimps, whose soft bodies are protected by the chalky exoskeletons that give them their name. Many have a pair of claws or pincers that can be used both for defence and to grip their prey. Some also have shells covered in sharp spines.

ECHINODERMS

Starfish, sea urchins and sea cucumbers are all types of echinoderm. Many parts of their bodies (including their mouthparts) have a five-point radial symmetry. Sea urchins are often covered in sharp spines that snap off in the skin of predators. Starfish use their arms to prise open shells and can regrow any arms that are bitten off by predators.

MOLLUSCS

The oceans are home to a bewildering variety of molluscs. Sea snails are protected by their hard shells and can withdraw completely inside them at any sign of danger. Some, like the cone snail, catch prey by firing venemous barbs. Bivalves have a hinged shell that they can snap shut and strong muscles that secure them safely inside.

Sea slugs, also known as nudibranchs, are some of the most colourful animals in the sea. These molluscs have no shells to protect them. Instead, their bright colours and vivid patterns warn predators that their skin is armed with stinging cells — obtained from eating sea anemones, their favourite food.

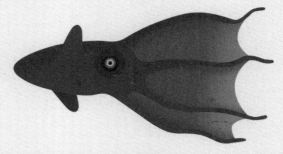

Cephalopods are a group of molluscs that include the octopuses, squid, nautiluses and cuttlefish. Many have sucker-covered tentacles to help them catch and hold their food, and a beak-like mouth that can deliver a venemous bite. If attacked, most cephalopods can release a cloud of dark ink from ink sacs between their gills to help them escape.

OCEAN LAYERS

THE OCEANS ARE EARTH'S BIGGEST HABITAT, holding over 90 per cent of the planet's water and covering more than three-quarters of its surface, yet scientists believe that we have explored only a tiny part of this amazing underwater kingdom. Like the dry land above, the ocean landscape is filled with towering mountains, huge valleys, erupting volcanoes and great open plains. It supports a greater variety of life than any other habitat and is where all life on Earth began, thousands of millions of years ago. There are creatures at every level – from the sunlit surface waters to the deepest, darkest depths of the abyss, thousands of metres below.

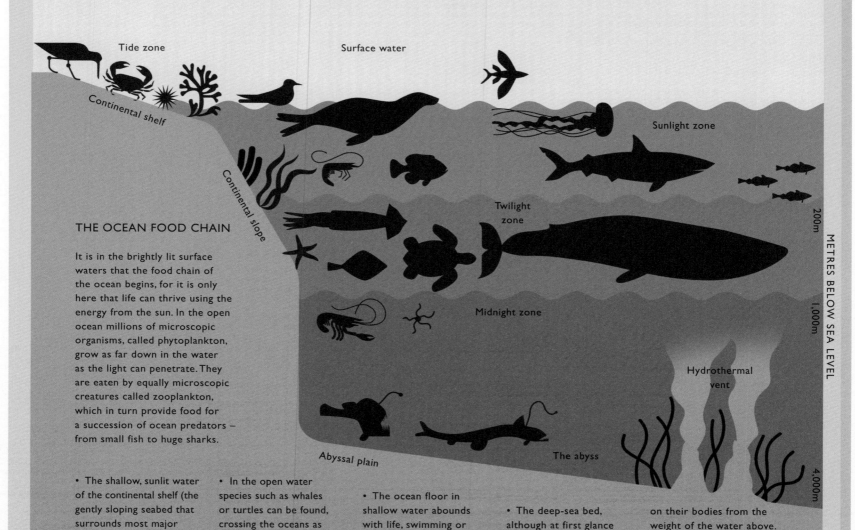

Tide zone

Surface water

Continental shelf

Sunlight zone

Continental slope

Twilight zone

THE OCEAN FOOD CHAIN

It is in the brightly lit surface waters that the food chain of the ocean begins, for it is only here that life can thrive using the energy from the sun. In the open ocean millions of microscopic organisms, called phytoplankton, grow as far down in the water as the light can penetrate. They are eaten by equally microscopic creatures called zooplankton, which in turn provide food for a succession of ocean predators – from small fish to huge sharks.

Midnight zone

Hydrothermal vent

Abyssal plain

The abyss

200m

1,000m

4,000m

METRES BELOW SEA LEVEL

• The shallow, sunlit water of the continental shelf (the gently sloping seabed that surrounds most major landmasses) supports most of the oceans' wildlife for it is here that there is the most food. Algae, seagrass and tiny creatures provide food for huge shoals of fish and all manner of molluscs and crustaceans.

• In the open water species such as whales or turtles can be found, crossing the oceans as they migrate between their feeding and breeding grounds. Exceptional swimmers such as dolphins often roam in search of food, while at the surface, jellyfish are borne along by the currents.

• The ocean floor in shallow water abounds with life, swimming or crawling over the seabed or burrowing through it in search of food. Many creatures here are scavengers, feeding on dead matter that drifts down from the upper layers like marine snow.

• The deep-sea bed, although at first glance inhospitable, is actually one of the most stable environments on Earth. The creatures that live here have evolved to survive the extreme dark and cold as well as the intense pressure exerted on their bodies from the weight of the water above.
• Hydrothermal vents on some parts of the sea bed support their own mini ecosystem where creatures found nowhere else use the energy released by volcanic activity in the Earth's core.

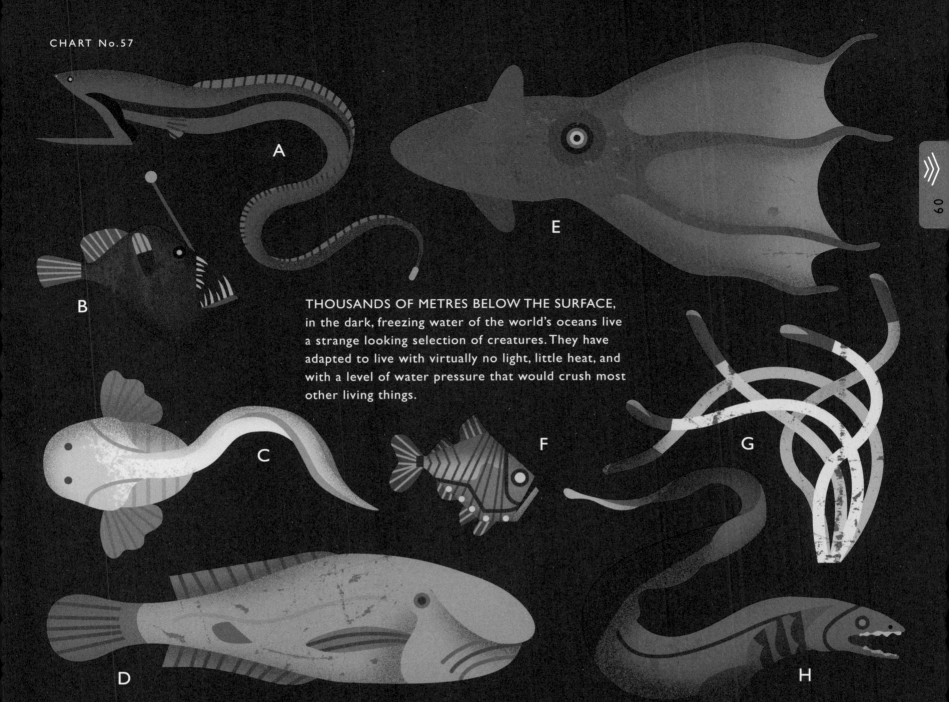

THOUSANDS OF METRES BELOW THE SURFACE, in the dark, freezing water of the world's oceans live a strange looking selection of creatures. They have adapted to live with virtually no light, little heat, and with a level of water pressure that would crush most other living things.

CREATURES OF THE DEEP

A. Pelican eel – Also known as the gulper eel, this fish's most notable feature is its huge mouth, which is much larger than its body. It can open its loosely-hinged jaws wide enough to swallow fish much bigger than itself.

B. Humpback anglerfish – One of the strangest creatures at these depths, this anglerfish has a bioluminescent, or light-producing, lure attached to its head. It uses this to attract food in the freezing, pitch-dark water where it lives, nearly 2,000 metres below the surface. It is found in all the world's oceans.

C. Deep-sea snailfish –Holding the record for the deepest dwelling fish, this recently discovered species was found during an expedition 8,000 metres below the surface of the Pacific Ocean, in the Marianas Trench. Its ghostly, tadpole-like body is virtually transparent.

D. Blobfish – The blobfish floats just above the ocean floor waiting for food to float close by. It is made of a jelly-like substance and has virtually no muscles in its body at all.

E. Vampire squid – The body of this deep-sea cephalopod is almost entirely covered in light-producing cells, called photophores, which enable it to emit disorientating flashes of light to deter would-be predators.

F. Marine hatchet-fish – These small, peculiarly shaped fish have delicate silvery scales and enormous eyes that can focus even in the faintest light. Their eyes are directed upwards so they can see prey moving overhead, silhouetted against the brighter surface water. Hatchet-fish are often found in shoals and use rows of lights along their bodies.

G. Giant tube worm – Found living near thermal vents on the floor of the Pacific Ocean, these marine invertebrates can reach lengths of over 2 metres. They have no digestive tract, but instead use bacteria in their bodies to turn compounds absorbed from seawater (such as oxygen, hydrogen sulfide and carbon dioxide) into organic molecules on which they feed. Entire mini-ecosystems exist around the vents.

H. Frilled shark – Highly specialised for life in the deep oceans, the frilled shark, with its eel-like body and flexible jaw, belongs to one of the oldest surviving shark lineages that has lived on Earth for nearly 100 million years. This 2-metre beast feeds on soft-bodied animals, such as squid, as well as fish.

Focus on Nature:
THE BLUE-RINGED OCTOPUS

A MEMBER OF THE CEPHALOPOD CLASS, THE GREATER BLUE-RINGED OCTOPUS IS SMALL, BEAUTIFUL AND DEADLY. It inhabits the coral reefs of the Pacific and Indian Oceans and its venomous bite can kill a human in less than 15 minutes. The first octopuses evolved about 150 million years ago. As well as being able to change colour, they can also change the shape of their bodies, helping them to squeeze into small crevices in the reef rock where they spend much of their time hiding. The female only lays one clutch of about 50 eggs in her lifetime. Once her eggs have hatched, she will die.

A. **Chromatophore cells** – Cells in the skin change colour to camouflage the octopus. or show its warning colours (yellow and with blue rings) to frighten off any would-be predators.

B. **Horny beak** – Used to pierce crabs' and shrimps' shells.

C. **Two large eyes** – It has a well-developed sense of sight.

D. **Large brain** – It is one of the most intelligent invertebrates.

E. **Siphon** – This 'funnel' sucks water into the mantle cavity, then shoots it out to propel the animal forward.

F. **Body cavity** – Or 'mantle'.

G. Eight arms or **tentacles** – Each one has two rows of suction cups, or suckers. A lost tentacle can regrow in a matter of weeks.

H. **Suckers** – Along the tentacles, suckers help the creature to grip rocks and hold onto its prey.

WARNING COLOURS

Like the blue-ringed octopus, many other creatures use colour and high-contrast patterns to warn potential predators that they are dangerous or foul to eat. This is called warning colouration or aposematism. The most common warning colours are red, yellow, black and white. The brighter and more conspicuous the creature, the more dangerous or foul-tasting it usually is.

Poison dart frog

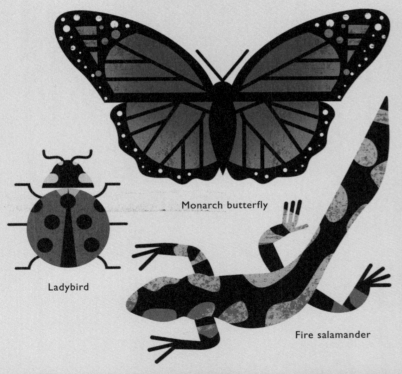

Monarch butterfly

Skunk

Coral snake

Ladybird

Fire salamander

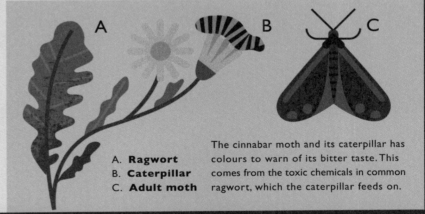

A

B

C

A. **Ragwort**
B. **Caterpillar**
C. **Adult moth**

The cinnabar moth and its caterpillar has colours to warn of its bitter taste. This comes from the toxic chemicals in common ragwort, which the caterpillar feeds on.

CLEVER IMPOSTERS

Bee

Hoverfly

Some creatures have evolved warning colouration even though they do not possess any other secondary defence mechanisms such as stings or a horrid taste. By mimicking more dangerous creatures they too gain protection from would-be predators. This form of imitation is called Batesian mimicry.

Another form of mimicry, Müllerian mimicry, explains why many different species may share the same sort of aposematic colouring to warn off attackers.

These different kinds of beetle, for example, all taste horrid and are all patterned in bright red and black, so many species gain protection from the lesson learnt when a predator attacks just one.

Froghopper bug

Italian striped-bug

Soldier beetle

Firebug

BATESIAN MIMICRY

MÜLLERIAN MIMICRY

63

THE ART OF DISGUISE

ONE INTERESTING FORM OF CAMOUFLAGE AMONG ANIMALS RELIES ON THE ART OF DISGUISE RATHER THAN CONCEALMENT, where certain creatures have evolved colours, forms and postures that help them to look like inanimate objects. Some, like the leaf mantis, use this technique to help them catch their prey, but it is more commonly seen as a form of defence against predation than a means to a quick meal. This form of camouflage, known as **mimesis**, is very common among insects where strangely shaped wings, fleshy lumps and bumps and other bodily features help a host of different species disguise themselves variously as anything from a dead leaf, twig or row of thorns to a bird dropping!

KEY TO SPECIES

A. **Stick insect** – In the wild these familiar pets freeze into position to look just like twigs. The longest stick insects can reach over 56 centimetres.

B. **Dead leaf butterfly** – As its name suggests, this butterfly closes its wings over its back to resemble a dead leaf. Normally, such disguises require the creatures to remain perfectly still for the trick to work, but in this case the disguise is taken one step further by the addition of movement, with the butterfly swaying slowly from side to side like a dead leaf blowing in the wind.

C. **Moss caterpillar** – These insects have bodies covered in hairy protrusions that make them look like moss. The pupa's cocoon is also camouflaged with numerous spikes and other projections.

D. **Thorn bugs** – These will cluster together along the stems of a plant to reinforce their thorny disguise.

E. **Crab spider** – Tucking its long legs beneath its body enables this spider to look just like a bird dropping and go unnoticed.

F. **Leaf mantis** – These leaf mimics are found in tropical forests where they are easily mistaken for part of the plant on which they live. Some species imitate dead leaves instead.

E

D

F

EYE-EYE!

A mimicking tactic used by predated species (those that are preyed upon by other creatures), particularly insects, is the use of eyespots which can make an otherwise defenceless creature look like a much bigger and more dangerous animal.

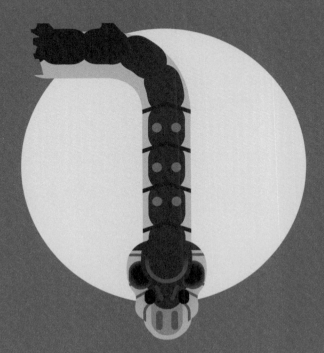

This **hawkmoth caterpillar** will expand the lower segments of its body to give its tail the appearance of a snake, complete with menacing eye-like markings. It will extend the mimicry even further by striking out at potential predators in an attempt to frighten them away.

The bold eyespots on the hind wings of this **eyed hawkmoth** make it look like the head of a much bigger animal, especially when the moth sits in a head-down position as shown here. Many species of moth and butterfly have similar eyespots which they flash at potential attackers to frighten them away.

BUTTERFLIES AND MOTHS

WITH OVER 165,000 IDENTIFIED SPECIES between them, butterflies and moths are some of the most incredible insects in the world. Belonging to the order Lepidoptera they have wings covered in minute overlapping scales, a long coiled feeding tube instead of a mouth and are often brightly coloured or patterned.

All species lay eggs that hatch into larvae, called **caterpillars**. When they are ready to begin their adult lives, the caterpillars build cocoons and eventually emerge as adult insects through a process known as **metamorphosis**.

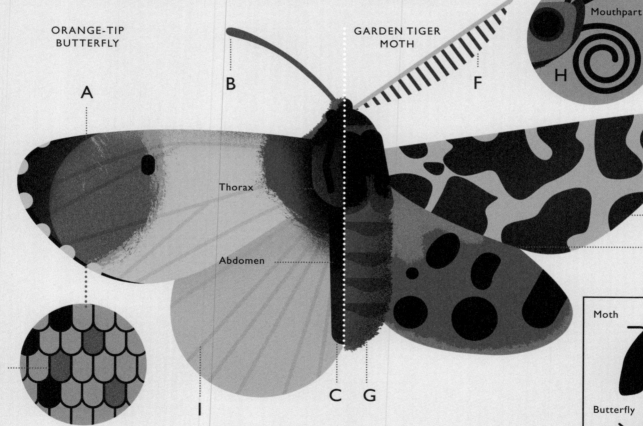

ORANGE-TIP BUTTERFLY

GARDEN TIGER MOTH

Mouthpart

A

B

F

H

Thorax

D

E

Abdomen

J

C   G

I

Moth

Butterfly

HOW CAN YOU TELL A BUTTERFLY FROM A MOTH?

Though there are exceptions, in general butterflies are more brightly coloured than moths and fly about in the day. They also have thin antennae, often ending in a ball or club. Moths are more typically nocturnal, have feathery antennae and are often drably coloured.

BUTTERFLY
A. **Wings** – Often brightly coloured or patterned.

B. **Club-ended antennae**

C. **Smooth abdomen**

MOTH
D. **Drab colour** – Often helps with camouflage,

E. **Front** and **back wings** – Hooked together; often longer and thinner than a butterfly's.

F. **Feathery antennae** – The large surface area of the antennae picks up the scent of a mate.

G. **Hairy body**

BOTH
H. **Proboscis** – Feeding tube; rolled up unless in use.

I. Network of **rigid veins** – Strengthens the wings.

J. Tiny overlapping **scales** on the wings – These contain coloured pigments or reflect coloured light.

RESTING
When butterflies are at rest they often hold their wings upright over their backs.
• The underside of their wings are often drab colours to help with camouflage.
• In contrast, moths usually fold their wings flat over their back or hold them open when resting.

BUTTERFLIES

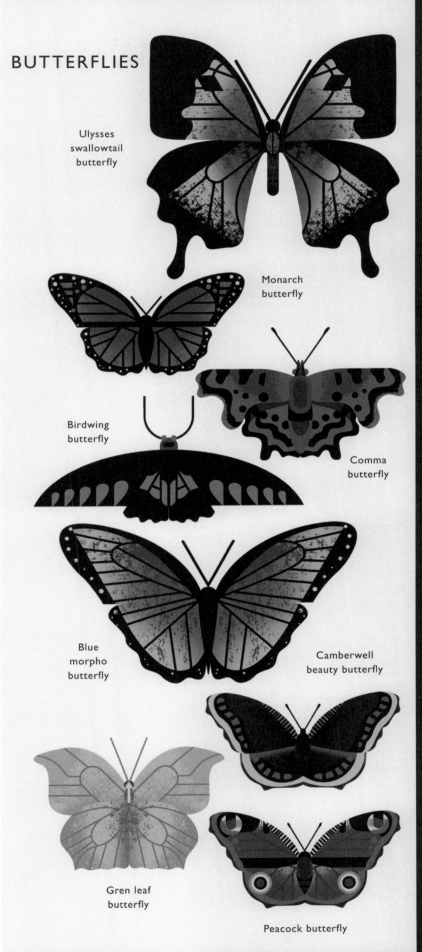

Ulysses swallowtail butterfly

Monarch butterfly

Birdwing butterfly

Comma butterfly

Blue morpho butterfly

Camberwell beauty butterfly

Gren leaf butterfly

Peacock butterfly

MOTHS

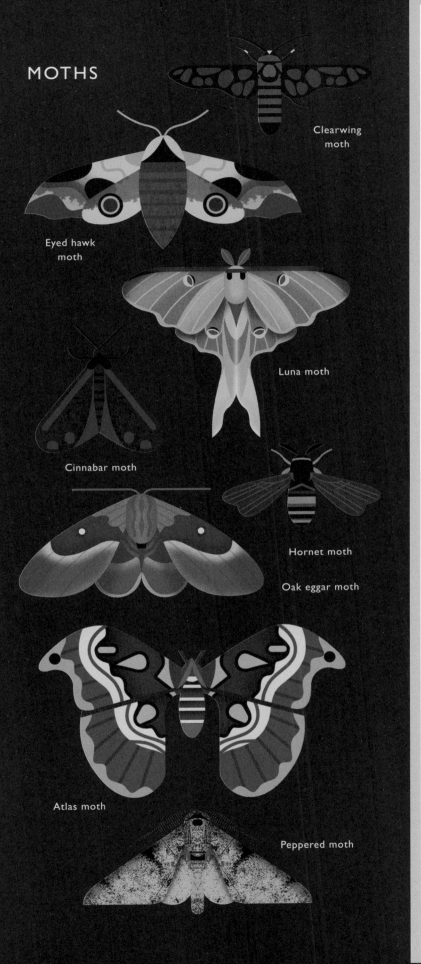

Clearwing moth

Eyed hawk moth

Luna moth

Cinnabar moth

Hornet moth

Oak eggar moth

Atlas moth

Peppered moth

TWO LIVES IN ONE

THE PROCESS BY WHICH ANIMALS DRAMATICALLY CHANGE FORM AS THEY GROW IS CALLED **METAMORPHOSIS**. This transformation can happen gradually as an animal grows or rapidly when it reaches a certain age. By having this two-stage life, an animal can make use of more than one food source and sometimes more than one habitat, so improving their chances of survival.

Butterflies, moths and many other insects undergo **complete metamorphosis**. They hatch from eggs into **larvae**, for example caterpillars or maggots, and then undergo a drastic change into their adult form during a resting stage called pupation. During this stage their bodies are broken down and rearranged inside a protective case, or **cocoon**.

A. **Eggs** – Often laid on the underside of leaves
B. **Caterpillar** – Eats plants
C. **Pupa** – Also known as a cocoon or chrysalis
D. **Emerging butterfly** – Comes out damp
E. **Adult butterfly** – Drinks nectar

DRAGONFLY LIFE CYCLE

Some insects, such as dragonflies, grasshoppers and bugs, undergo **incomplete metamorphosis**.
• Their young look similar to their adult form and are called **nymphs**.
• They change gradually every time they moult, shedding their old skin along the way until they finally develop their wings and emerge as a fully fledged adult insect.

A. **Egg** – Laid in water
B. **Nymph** – Can take four years to reach adulthood
C. **Adult dragonfly**

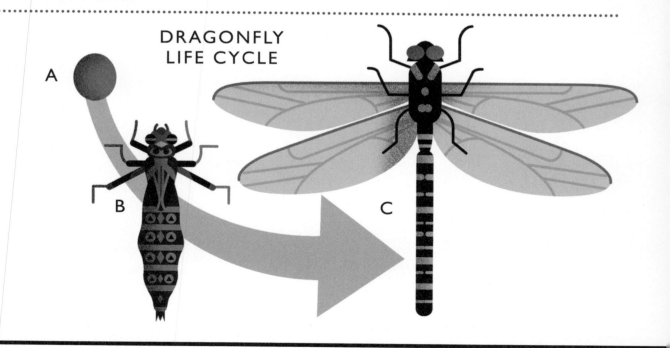

Some water-dwelling animals such as certain species of crustacean, echinoderm and amphibian also undergo metamorphosis. In the case of the common frog the eggs are laid in water as **spawn**.
• The young hatch as **tadpoles** and gradually transform into adult frogs over a number of weeks, developing lungs ready for life on land.

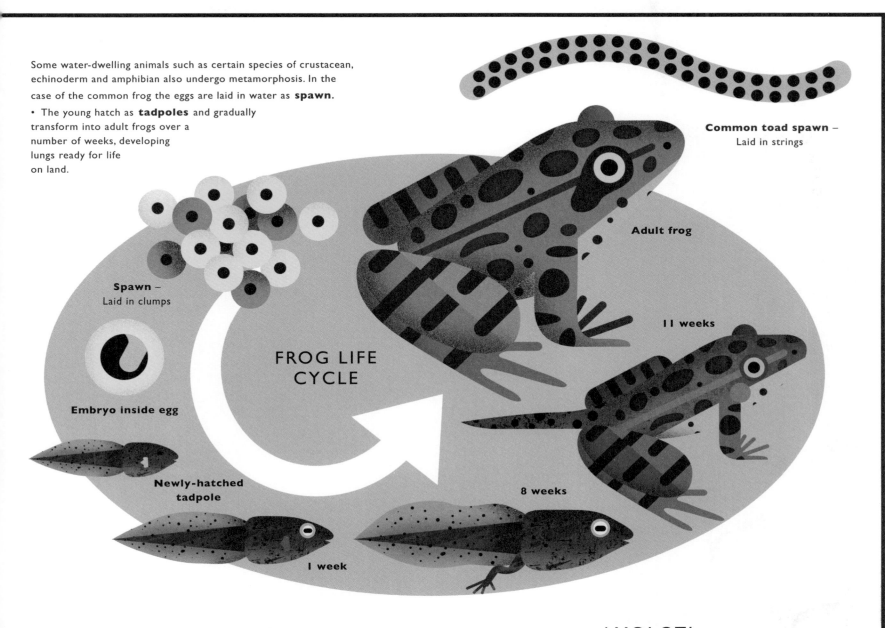

Common toad spawn – Laid in strings

Spawn – Laid in clumps

Embryo inside egg

FROG LIFE CYCLE

Adult frog

11 weeks

8 weeks

Newly-hatched tadpole

1 week

CRAB LIFE CYCLE

Crabs pass through a number of larval stages before reaching adulthood.
• One such stage, **zoea**, was once thought to be an entirely separate species.

Egg

Megalopa

Zoea

Juvenile crab

Adult crab

AXOLOTL

The curious axolotl, a type of salamander, cheats metamorphosis by retaining the appearance of a juvenile for its whole life.
• It only changes externlly into its adult form if the water in which it is living dries up.
• Like other salamanders, it can also regenerate its body parts, growing a leg or even an eye if the old one is lost through injury.

Gills

SURVIVING THE SEASONS

FOR LOTS OF CREATURES, FINDING FOOD DURING THE LONG, COLD MONTHS OF WINTER IS A CHALLENGE. Some animals may **migrate**, sometimes travelling long distances to places where food is plentiful. For others, the answer is to **hibernate**, building nests or dens to shelter in until warmer weather returns, conserving their energy by lowering their body temperature and slowing down their bodily systems.

• Many animals – like this **black bear** with her newborn cubs – prepare for hibernation by building up a store of food beforehand, eating as much as they can and storing the energy as fat in their bodies to last them through the winter. Others make a physical store, hiding away a cache of nuts or seeds in readiness for the lean months ahead.

• Hibernating mammals grow thick coats of fur to help keep themselves warm, while many insects overwinter as pupae,

emerging only when the warmer days of spring arrive.

• The length of time a creature hibernates can last days, weeks or months depending on the species and the external conditions. Some creatures wake up periodically during their hibernation period, to enjoy a short period of warmth, to warm up their bodies by briefly moving about, or to eat a little food from their stores before going back to sleep again. Plants respond to these yearly changes too – deciduous trees lose their leaves as there is less light and water to enable photosynthesis to take place, and flowers die off as there are fewer birds and insects to pollinate them.

• Some creatures also hibernate through periods of extreme heat, and this is known as **aestivation**. Water-storing frogs for example, burrow deep beneath the desert sands, sealed in a cocoon made of special skin that allows them to remain moist. It may remain like this for as long as eight months.

A. **Black bear** – Like some other bear species, the female gives birth to her young during the hibernation period. Even though her eggs have been fertilised much earlier, the embryos will not begin to develop until their mother has entered her hibernation state. The cubs will remain in the den with their mother until the snow melts in spring, by which time she may have lost nearly half her body weight.

B. **Monarch butterfly** – Many insects hibernate during periods of extreme cold, sometimes in congregations of many hundreds of individuals. Butterflies such as the monarch will hibernate as part of their annual migration, clustering together in trees, caves or other protected places.

C. **Bat** – Bats that live in colder climates or higher altitudes hibernate when their insect prey becomes scarce. They can often be found clustered together, curled up like furry balls in the roofs of caves, hollow trees and abandoned buildings.

D. **Snail** – Some species retreat into their shells to survive either extreme cold or drought. To keep their bodies moist during hibernation they use a dried layer of mucus, called an **epiphragm**, to seal themselves in.

E. **Chipmunk** – Like other small mammals, it spends the summer building up a cache of nuts, seeds and berries to help them survive through the long winter months. During hibernation it will wake periodically to dip into its store and replenish its energy levels.

SNOW ZONE

ALPINE MEADOW

CLOUD FOREST

Journey through Nature:

ON TOP OF THE WORLD

THE HIMALAYAS ARE OFTEN REFERRED TO AS THE THIRD POLE OF THE EARTH. With their thousands of glaciers and annual snow melt, these mountains are the source of the ten biggest rivers in Asia and part of the climate regulation of our planet. The highest and longest mountain range on Earth, the Himalayas stretch for 1,500 miles, and include nine out of ten of the world's highest peaks, including Mount Everest, the highest of them all.

From the snow-covered heights to the lushly forested lower slopes, the wildlife of the Himalayas includes a great diversity of creatures, many of which are found nowhere else in the world. You can find out more about the creatures shown here by turning the page.

WHO LIVES HERE?

STEEPLY RISING 8,000 METRES OVER A DISTANCE OF JUST 2 KILOMETRES, the greatest mountain range on Earth supports many different ecosystems in its near vertical climb towards the sky. On the higher slopes plants and animals have adapted to their high-rise life coping, not just with falling temperatures (roughly 1°C for every 150 metre rise in altitude), but with a lack of oxygen, low moisture, biting winds and fierce radiation from the sun. Little vegetation can grow in the snow zone but wildlife still occurs here; creatures that have evolved to survive in this snowy wilderness, hunting, mating and raising their young on the roof of the world.

8,844.43m ········· SUMMIT

Glacier

5,600m ·········

Snow zone

4,800m ········· Tibetan Plateau

Alpine steppe

4,200m ········· Alpine meadow Treeline

3,800m ········· Sub-alpine scrub

CLOUD BELT

3,100m ·········

Coniferous forest

1,600m ·········

Broad-leaved forest

MOUNTAIN PLANTS

Mountain vegetation changes according to altitude. In the Himalayas, subtropical forest gives way to broad-leafed woodland as you move higher, then to dense conifers up to the treeline, where it becomes too cold and dry for trees to grow.
• At cloud level, forests are persistently shrouded in mist and are hung with orchids, liverworts, beard-mosses and lichens.
• Above cloud level, radiation is fierce, but it can be very cold and dry. Here, water-conserving plants like sedums thrive.
• In the snow zone, mosses and lichens are an important food source for grazing animals such as yak.
• The grasslands of the Tibetan Plateau form an alpine steppe where flocks of migrating birds rest on their journey.

A. **Himalayan brown bear** – This subspecies has woolly fur to keep it warm at high altitudes, and as it hibernates through the winter.

B. **Yak** – The yak's coat is so dense and matted that it can survive temperatures as low as -40°C. When no other food is available, it will live on mosses and lichens and eat snow to obtain water.

C. **Snow leopard** – This predator hunts above the treeline in summer where it must rely on its stealth and its camouflaging coat to catch its prey of yak calves, mountain sheep, and other small creatures.

D. **Tahr** – The goat-like tahr is superbly adapted to life on the high slopes, climbing and leaping across the rocky terrain with ease. Like many mountain mammals, it returns to the forests in winter.

E. **Bar-headed goose** – One of the world's highest-flying birds, these geese migrate across the Himalayas to breed on the Tibetan Plateau in summer.

F. **Apollo butterfly** – Found in mountainous habitats around the world, it lives at altitudes of 3,500 metres.

G. **Himalayan blue sheep** – Also known as the bharal, this mountain-grazer prefers to feed in the alpine meadows despite its great agility.

H. **Himalayan marmot** – This rodent digs deep burrows in the alpine meadows where its whole colony will hibernate in winter.

I. **Himalayan wolf** – A subspecies of the grey wolf, this elusive hunter will listen for marmots under the ground, pouncing on them when they leave their burrows.

J. **Pika** – This denizen of the Tibetan Plateau collects green plants in the summer and stores them to be used for winter food.

K. **Markhor** – During winter, the markhor moves from alpine grassland to lower slopes to eat leaves and twigs. The male's spectacular spiral horn can reach 1.6 metres.

L. **Himalayan monal** – Most commonly found inhabiting oak forests. The male has brilliant plumage; the female is a dull brown.

M. **Himalayan toad** – This amphibian inhabits mountain forest and scrub.

N. **Black-necked crane** – Cranes gather to breed on the Tibetan Plateau and forage daily for food for many hours.

O. **White-bellied musk deer** – Well adapted for high altitudes, these deer have broad toes to help them grip steep slopes.

P. **Red panda** – This tree-dwelling, raccoon-like creature spends much of its life in the temperate forests where it will make a nest lined with leaves in which to raise its young.

Q. **Satyr tragopan** – The male tragopan grows feathery horns and an elaborately coloured wattle to attract a female at the start of the breeding season.

THE LIFE OF A LOG

A TREE MAY LIVE FOR HUNDREDS OF YEARS BUT EVENTUALLY, AS WITH ALL LIVING THINGS, IT WILL DIE. Its end may be hastened by woodboring beetles and other invasive insects, by woodpeckers attacking its bark in search of a meal, or by fungi that will invade any wounds in its trunk, weakening the timber until the tree finally falls to the ground.

A new cast of creatures will then come to rely on the dead tree for food and shelter. Fungi of many types will soon colonise the decaying trunk, animals may shelter in its hollow core, and many invertebrates will make their homes among its crumbling bark, in turn attracting a host of insect-eaters.

After several years the tree trunk will disappear completely, the energy stored within it now returned to the soil to nourish a new generation of plants.

KEY TO SPECIES

A. **Woodlouse**
B. **Ladybird**
C. **Ant and larva**
D. **Honey fungus**
E. **Northern flicker**
F. **Bracket fungi**
G. **Porcupine**
H. **Earthworm**
I. **Oak seedling**
J. **Millipede**

CHART No.67

THE CHANG

THERE IS ONE SPECIES OF ANIMAL THAT HAS ALTERED THE FACE OF THE EARTH MORE THAN ANY OTHER. That species is *Homo sapiens* – the human being. Before the beginning of agriculture, about 10,000 years ago, small groups of humans wandered across large areas of land, hunting and gathering only enough food to stay alive. The number of humans on Earth was kept low because of the difficulty of finding food. Since then our population has greatly increased – with an explosion in the last 200 years that has seen our numbers grow from a billion to over 7 billion people, putting an ever-increasing strain on the natural world.

We are not the only creatures to shape our surroundings, but no other

ING PLANET

species has been so thorough or as widespread. Thanks to our intelligence and ingenuity, we can adapt and survive in almost all climates and habitats, controlling ever-widening tracts of land, competing with other living things for space and resources, and unfortunately polluting the land, air and water. While some creatures have learned to live alongside us, many others find it increasingly hard to survive.

The name *Homo sapiens* means 'wise person' and increasingly we are realising the vital importance of finding ways to protect our planet, preserving for future generations the many incredible habitats and the creatures that share this wonderful world we call 'home'.

Index